Donated by...

Geoffrey Engholm

JUN 4 - 1997

JOHN HEDGECOE'S NUDE AND PORTRAIT PHOTOGRAPHY

John Hedgecoe's Nude and Portrait Photography

Edited and designed by Mitchell Beazley International Ltd,
14–15 Manette Street, London W1V 5LB

© 1985 Mitchell Beazley Publishers
Text © 1985 Mitchell Beazley Publishers and John Hedgecoe
Photographs © 1978, 1979, 1980, 1982, 1983 and 1984 John Hedgecoe

Published by Simon and Schuster
A Division of Simon & Schuster, Inc.
Simon & Schuster Building
Rockefeller Center
1230 Avenue of the Americas
New York, New York 10020

1 2 3 4 5 6 7 8 9 10

Library of Congress Cataloging in Publication Data

Hedgecoe, John.
  John Hedgecoe's Nude and portrait photography.

  Includes index.
  1. Photography of the nude.   2. Photography—Portraits
3. Glamour photography.   I. Title.   II. Title: Nude and
portrait photography.
TR674.H44 1985   778.9′2   84–27753
ISBN 0–671–50892–X

Typeset and prepared by
Servis Filmsetting Ltd, Manchester
Reproduction by Chelmer Litho Reproductions, Maldon
Printed and bound in Italy by New Inter Litho SPA, Milan

Editor	John Smith
Art editor	Zoë Davenport
Production	Peter Phillips
	Androulla Pavlou
Artist	Stan North

JOHN HEDGECOE'S NUDE AND PORTRAIT PHOTOGRAPHY

by John Hedgecoe

SIMON AND SCHUSTER
NEW YORK

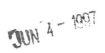

CONTENTS

INTRODUCTION

I have always believed in the broadest possible approach to nude and glamor photography, embracing every setting from studio to saltmarsh, every tincture of mood from pensively romantic to brassily flirtatious. This book reflects such diversity. I have planned it not as a step-by-step photo course, but as a sourcebook of techniques and ideas that should be useful to anyone who enjoys photographing women (even just one or two specific women), however humbly or ambitiously.

Dismiss from your mind the cliché of a hard-bitten photographer shouting orders at a shivering model. My starting point is a two-way sympathy: with the beginner summoning the courage to ask the girl next door to model for him (or her); and with the girl herself, when

she is asked to adopt unfamiliar poses or expressions or to shed garments.

If understanding and tact are vital qualities in this field, another, equally important, is the ability to use and control light – be it daylight, portable flash or more sophisticated studio lighting. I cover these aspects thoroughly, aware that the novice can easily be intimidated by them.

Above all, you must learn to realize the full potential of your imagination, which I hope the examples in this book will stimulate. Let your creativity grow with your camera handling and lighting skills. Don't be afraid of your own ideas. They are probably as valid as mine or anyone else's.

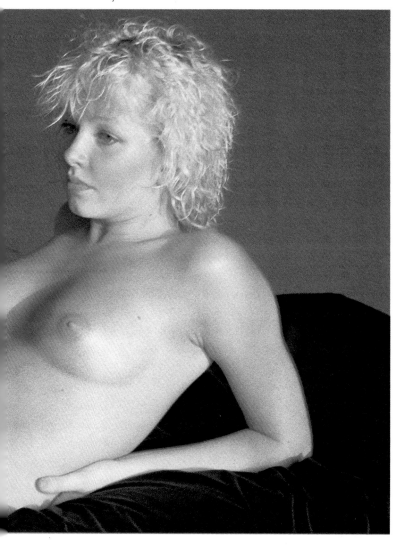

CHOOSING EQUIPMENT

You will usually get more enjoyment out of photography if the equipment you acquire extends slightly beyond your current needs. This way, you can be sure of accommodating growing skills and ambitions. Thoroughly research all the types and brands available, even if you are buying a relatively minor item, such as a cable release or lens hood. When choosing a camera body, make sure that it can be be fitted with all the lenses and the accessories you may one day wish to acquire. Never underestimate the importance of proper equipment care. Have your camera overhauled occasionally, to ensure that moving parts are working accurately and reliably.

● **A 35mm SLR camera** is the most versatile choice. Very portable and easy to use, it offers a lens-eye view, through-the-lens (TTL) metering and can be fitted with a wide range of lenses and accessories.

● **Automatic cameras** take exposure judgments out of your hands, allowing you to concentrate on composing the image and directing the model. However, complete reliance on automation often sacrifices creativity to convenience, and may prevent beginners from acquiring important photographic skills. The best choice is undoubtedly an automatic 35mm camera with manual override.

● **Compact 35mm cameras** do not have the range of controls available with 35mm SLRs. Moreover, their fixed wide-angle lens (usually around 35mm or 40mm) is unsuitable for full-frame portraiture. However, compact cameras allow you to take pictures quickly and inconspicuously, and are therefore useful for candid photography. It is worth carrying a compact at all times, to make visual notes whenever you come across potential locations.

● **Medium-format** (or rollfilm) cameras are much more expensive than 35mm SLR cameras, but offer an image quality suited to commercial reproduction. (See pages 16–17)

● **Accessories** extend your creative range – but only if they genuinely enable you to use your existing equipment more

creatively or conveniently, or with less risk of damage. Resist the temptation to accumulate gadgetry for its own sake. Keeping your outfit down to a minimum is especially important on location: excess baggage will merely sap your strength and increase the likelihood of leaving something behind.

BUYING HINTS
● **Keep up-to-date** with advances in photo technology – but don't assume that the latest equipment is necessarily the most versatile or reliable.

● **Top manufacturers** of cameras – such as Canon, Minolta, Nikon, Olympus, Pentax, Hasselblad and Bronica – can always be relied upon for quality, and for good after-sales service.

● **Photo magazines** are a useful source of guidance. Read their comparative test reports on cameras, lenses and other equipment before making a major purchase.

● **Avoid relying** entirely on advice from your local dealer. It is preferable to talk to practicing photographers.

● **Avoid peak-hour shopping.** When a camera shop is crowded, you will probably not get the detailed attention you need and may be rushed into making a choice.

● **Feel** is more important than looks. Handle equipment, and try all the settings, before you purchase.

● **Rent an expensive item** to try it out before making a final decision to buy.

● **Don't trade in** your old camera just for the sake of a marginal saving. Keep it as a second camera, which you can load with an alternative choice of film.

● **A special price** for a package consisting of camera, tripod and flashgun may seem attractive. However, the flash is usually a low-powered unit without a bounce head, and the tripod insufficiently robust.

● **When budgeting** for a new camera, take into account the cost of replacing any incompatible lenses and accessories you own. Even replacing filters can involve considerable expense.

● **Buying secondhand** is a good way to acquire almost new, quality equipment. Preferably buy from a dealer, who will give you a guarantee. If you do decide to buy privately, you are more likely to get a good deal from an amateur who has hardly used his equipment than from a professional who has subjected the item to a lot of use over a short period. Never buy a camera with burred screw heads, which may indicate a clumsy repair. Good-quality medium-format cameras can often be bought secondhand at low prices; but make sure that compatible films are still available.

EQUIPMENT CARE
● **Keep each item** in its own place so that you will quickly notice if anything is missing.

● **Store equipment** in a cool, dry place, free from dust.

● **Replace batteries** regularly, and remove them when equipment is out of use.

● **Never force the controls** of your camera if a moving part jams.

● **Note the serial numbers** of all equipment in case of loss or theft.

● **Clean cameras** at least once a month: use a blower brush to remove dust from the inside, with the shutter open on its B setting.

● **Avoid lens cloths.** Instead, use a rolled-up lens tissue to brush away loose particles. Don't clean lenses too often or the elements may become scratched. Store with front and rear caps in place.

RENTING EQUIPMENT
● **Renting** is a sensible way to gain access to expensive equipment for occasional use. However, renting a small item for more than two or three days may be less economic than buying the item secondhand.

● **A deposit** to the value of the equipment borrowed will normally be required. You will also be asked to take out insurance.

● **A local dealer** who also operates a rental service is worth cultivating. You may even be able to borrow items from secondhand stock at a small charge.

● **35mm camera accessories** compatible with your own camera body may not be available for rental. Many companies only supply Nikon or Canon equipment.

● **Some retailers** with a rental department will deduct the rental charge if you decide to buy the item (or equivalent new equipment) within a specified period of returning it.

● **Lighting kits** for hire usually come with stands, barndoors and a carrying case. Spare bulbs are included with tungsten kits. Always return a blown bulb or you may be charged for it. Check whether safety filters are included: these prevent a dangerous burst of glass when a bulb blows, and are often blue-coated to convert tungsten lighting for daylight film.

● **Flash meters**, color temperature meters, background stands and portable generators can be hired for studio sessions.

BUILDING AN SLR OUTFIT

1. SLR camera. When making your choice, important factors are: ease of use, the range of compatible lenses and accessories, the range of shutter speeds and film speeds, the automation system, and the viewfinder display. Do not sacrifice important features for the sake of a 1/2000 shutter speed, which is seldom needed in glamor photography. Choose aperture-priority automation in preference to shutter-priority: by setting the aperture manually you can more easily control depth of field. An exposure compensation dial with half-stop or one-third-stop graduations provides more control. If you find lights in the viewfinder distracting, choose a needle display, not an LED (light-emitting diode) display. Some photographers consider it essential to have a depth-of-field preview button, which gives you a visual check on the depth of field at any aperture.

2. Tripod. Not only avoids camera shake, but also makes it easier to control viewpoint, subject and lighting accurately. Avoid the temptation to economize with a lightweight model. Check stability at all heights before buying, and make sure the locks are strong.

3. Cable release. Choose one at least 10ins (25cm) long.

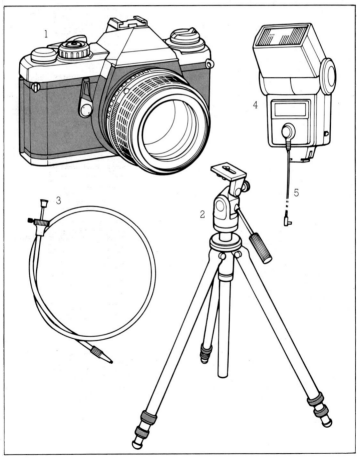

4. Portable flashgun. By far the least expensive and most portable type of artificial lighting. Strengths vary, though not in relation to size. Choose the most powerful you can afford, to increase your scope for bouncing the light; for this, a tilt head is virtually essential. Automatic units are programmed by dialling in the film speed and aperture required. With a 'dedicated' unit, flash exposures are controlled by the camera's TTL meter. (See also pages 18–19)

5. Sync lead. Allows you to use a flash unit off-camera (either handheld or on a bracket).

6. Handheld light meter. Simplifies exposure judgments in difficult lighting. Most types, unlike TTL meters in cameras, allow you to read incident light as well as reflected light (see page 32). For this purpose a diffusing dome is provided, which extends the meter's acceptance range. Selenium-cell meters need no batteries, but are less accurate in low light than cadmium sulphide (CdS) or silicon meters.

7. Lenses. In addition to a standard 50mm or 55mm lens, you will usually need at least one long-focus lens (preferably in the range, 85–150mm) and one wide-angle lens (28mm is a good choice). Lenses produced by the major camera manufacturers are a safer buy than less expensive lenses from independent firms, which may be inferior in definition, contrast and control of optical aberrations. 'Fast' lenses – that is, those with a wide maximum aperture relative to their focal length – give you more scope for reducing depth of field to blur a confusing background or for setting a fast shutter speed in dim light. However, fast lenses are heavier and more expensive than ordinary lenses. (See also pages 12–13)

8. Cleaning kit. Minimum equipment consists of a blower brush to remove dust, plus lens tissues to wipe optical surfaces.

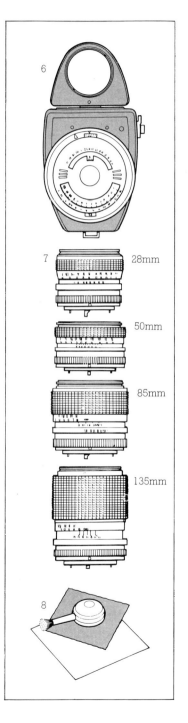

11

SLR LENSES

◀ **A standard lens** (that is, with a focal length somewhere between 45mm and 55mm) is excellent for full-length shots, especially on location. If you stop down to f/22, depth of field extends from 6 feet to infinity, revealing the setting in sharp detail. However, standard lenses also have the widest apertures (often f/1.7, sometimes f/1.2); this gives you great scope for opening up the aperture to blur a distracting background, cope with dim light or set a fast shutter speed to freeze movement.

◀ **Wide-angle lenses** have a broad angle of view and extensive depth of field, and can thus provide a generous view of the model's context, with both distant features and details only a few feet from the camera kept equally sharp. Focusing is less critical than with longer lenses. A 35mm or 28mm lens is the best choice, although you can use shorter lenses for distortion effects. Indoors, when you want to show more of a room than a standard lens would permit, a wide-angle lens is virtually essential. In the studio, however, you may find it difficult to exclude the edges of background paper.

The picture, left, was taken with a 35mm lens from the same viewpoint as the standard lens picture above it. Note how the vertical sides of the house converge. Because a wide-angle lens exaggerates perspective, such distortions are inevitable when you tilt the camera to take in the top of a building. One way to avoid them is to use a special shift lens, as I did for the image, left. Although expensive, a shift lens is a worthwhile investment if you plan to specialize in architectural settings.

▶ **Telephoto lenses** allow you to obtain a head-and-shoulders framing without crowding the model. Moreover, the shallow depth of field makes it easy to blur a confusing background. The most useful telephoto lenses for portraiture are those with focal lengths between 80mm and 135mm; you can use them even in rooms that are less than spacious, and they allow you to remain in conversational contact with the model. Lenses in the range 80mm to 105mm give a flattering perspective to the face.

▶ **Zoom lenses** – at least, the more expensive types – are now catching up in optical performance with fixed lenses. For glamor photography, a portrait zoom (say, 75–150mm) or long-focus zoom (80–200mm) is normally more useful than a wide-angle/portrait zoom (35–70mm). Remember that zoom lenses are heavier than fixed lenses, and may have a smaller maximum aperture. This picture (right) shows a unique zoom feature – the dynamic effect created when you change the focal length setting during exposure.

▶ **Special-effect lenses** have a limited though perfectly valid application in nude and glamor photography. They are too expensive to buy for merely occasional use, but it is fun to hire one for a day of experiment. This picture (right) was taken with an 8mm fisheye lens which produces circular, distorted images.

SLR ACCESSORIES

1. Camera case. A metal case offers best protection. The shiny aluminum type keeps camera and lenses cool in hot weather.

2. Lens hoods. Designed to eliminate flare. The shorter the focal length of the lens, the shallower the hood required.

3. Screw-in filters. Most useful are a skylight filter to reduce haze and a polarizing filter to cut reflections

from shiny surfaces and darken blue skies. A skylight filter may be left permanently over the lens to protect its front element.

4. System filters. Square plastic special-effects filters, which attach to the camera via a holder, are more economical than glass.

5. Light box. Facilitates sorting slides. Use it with a 4× or 8× magnifier and viewpack.

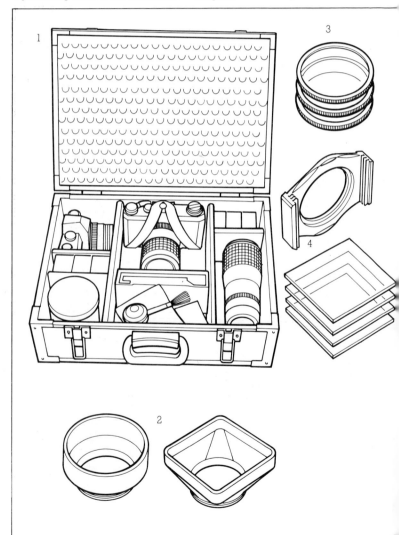

6. 2× teleconverter. Doubles the effective focal length of any prime lens. Cheaper teleconverters impair image quality; for best results, choose a converter that is specially matched to the lens.

7. Lens cases. Hard leather cases give better protection than pouches. They are useful if you are traveling light with a soft gadget bag, in which equipment might knock together.

8. Motordrive. A motordrive or autowind prevents your having to take your eye from the viewfinder between shots. A motordrive's capacity for continuous sequences at one to five frames per second is useful for capturing movement or fleeting expressions.

9. G-clamps. For supporting backgrounds, lights or props. Also of use: elastic luggage straps, gaffer tape, fishing line.

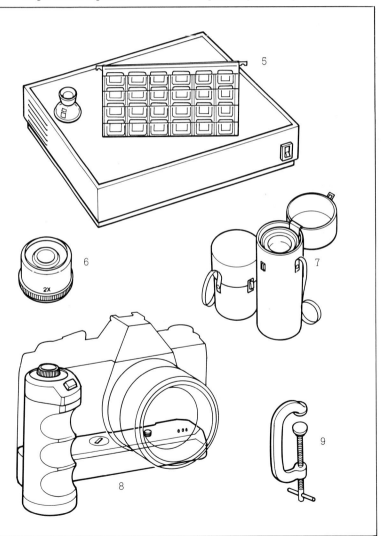

MEDIUM-FORMAT CAMERAS

Much favored by professional photographers (especially in the studio), medium-format cameras are almost as portable and versatile as the 35mm SLR, yet produce much larger negatives or transparencies on rollfilm, with a corresponding gain in image quality. SLR versions have superseded TLR (twin-lens reflex). Some models offer complete interchangeability of lenses, viewfinders, focusing screens and film backs. A medium-format camera is a big investment; however, mechanical and optical components are of superb quality and should last a lifetime.

● **The most popular format** for 120 rollfilm is $2\frac{1}{4} \times 2\frac{1}{4}$ins (6 × 6cm), which eliminates the need for turning the camera. Also available are: $2\frac{1}{4} \times 1\frac{3}{4}$ins (6 × 4.5cm), $2\frac{1}{4} \times 2\frac{3}{4}$ins (6 × 7cm) and $2\frac{1}{4} \times 3\frac{1}{2}$ins (6 × 9cm). Some cameras accept more than one format. 220 film is twice the length of 120, but with a narrower range of emulsions.

● **Shutters** may be the focal-plane type inside the body (as with most 35mm cameras) or the leaf type inside the lens. With leaf shutters, flash can be synchronized with all speeds.

● **Lenses** are more expensive than their 35mm equivalents and are available in a smaller range of focal lengths. They can only be used with the camera for which they are manufactured. The standard lens is 75mm or 80mm for 6 × 4.5 and 6 × 6 cameras, 100mm or 105mm for 6 × 7. Other popular 6 × 6 lenses range from 250mm long-focus to 40mm wide-angle; a typical portrait lens is 150mm.

▼ **The Hasselblad 500C/M** shows the construction of a traditional, manually operated waist-level SLR.
1. Film advance (to first frame)
2. Film magazine
3. Darkslide (protects film from light when magazine is removed)
4. Film winding crank
5. Hood
6. Viewing screen
7. Shutter release
8. Lens

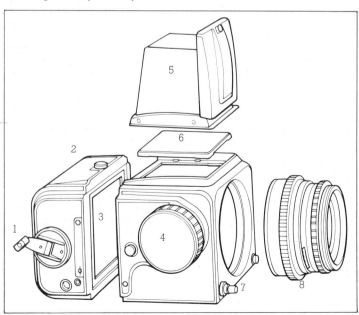

▲ **The Zenza Bronica ETRS**
(4.5 × 6) has aperture-priority
automation with an LED viewfinder
display. A 'speed-grip', with a
coupled shutter release and film
advance, simplifies picture-taking.
The camera is shown with eye-
level viewfinder and lens hood.

▲ **The Pentax 6 × 7** is unique in
being a scaled-up version of the
35mm SLR design, which makes it
quick and easy to use. Unlike most
other rollfilm cameras, it has an
instant-return mirror: this means
the viewfinder image reappears as
soon as the shutter has closed.

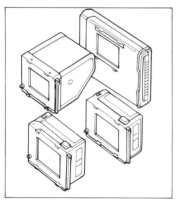

▲ **Film magazines** that are interchangeable enable you to switch
in mid-roll, in daylight, from one
film type to another – for example
from black-and-white to color. A
preloaded back is an advantage
when you want to change films
quickly. Of special use to studio
photographers is the Polaroid
instant-film back, which allows you
to preview composition, focusing
and lighting before switching to
rollfilm for the actual picture. An
interchangeable back adds to cost;
for this reason, some cameras are
sold in two versions – with and
without this facility.

▲ **Waist-level viewfinders**
normally have a flip-up magnifier
for focusing of the central image
area. The hood stores compactly
when collapsed. The absence of a
pentaprism makes the viewfinder
image reversed from left to right.
This gives an upside-down view
when you turn the camera for a
vertical-format image. To solve
this problem, one 6 × 7 model has
a rotating film magazine. Eye-level
pentaprism viewfinders are
available for all cameras. Since
holding a rollfilm camera at eye
level can be tiring, some
photographers use a pistol grip.

BUILDING A FLASH OUTFIT

A good-quality automatic flash unit, with a range of accessories, makes an excellent introduction to studio lighting – provided that it has a guide number of at least 60 (feet/ISO 100). The guide number of a sophisticated unit may be 140 or more. If your flashgun is underpowered, you may sacrifice the ability to light a generously framed full-length portrait, to set a small aperture for extended depth of field, or to bounce the flash, which requires two to four stops more exposure.

● **Recycling.** Today's more advanced units are thyristorized, which means that unused power after one flash is stored for the next flash. This can cut recycling time to a fraction of a second.

● **Range of apertures.** Medium-power units usually have a choice of only two stops, whereas more advanced units may have four or more. The greater the range of apertures, the more control you have over depth of field. A wide aperture reduces the power, and hence accelerates the recycling time; this is an advantage when you use flash with a motordrive.

● **Angle of illumination.** With most flashguns, this is 50°. Coverage can be extended by a diffuser (built-in or a separate accessory). Zoom heads offer both wide-angle and telephoto coverage.

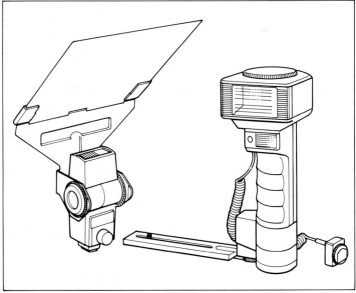

▲ **A clip-on reflecting screen** is an accessory for automatic units with a bounce head. Because the sensor under the flash head continues to measure light reaching the subject, no exposure compensation is necessary. An optional remote sensor which you attach to the camera gives accurate exposures with off-camera flash.

▲ **A hammerhead flashgun** has a barrel which serves as a grip, as well as containing batteries; it is attached to the camera by a bracket. The model shown here has a guide number of 140. Beneath the bounce head is a secondary fixed head, which provides fill-in lighting for portraiture, to remove shadows under nose and chin.

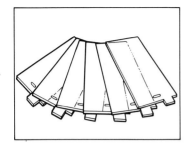

▲ **A filter kit** for a flashgun typically includes color filters, a UV filter, a conversion filter for use with tungsten film and an ND filter. These attach to the flash head by an adapter.

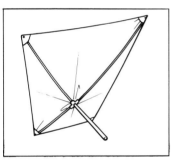

▲ **Folding white reflectors** for softening light are available commercially. However, you can easily improvise reflectors using white cardboard or polystyrene, white fabric, or cardboard covered with kitchen foil.

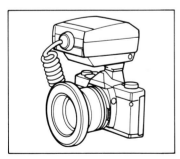

▲ **A ring flash** is a circular flash tube that fits over the lens barrel. It provides soft, shadowless frontal lighting, avoiding the need for cumbersome multiple-lamp setups.

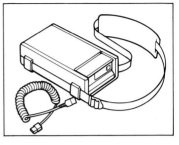

▲ **A high-voltage power pack,** available for some flashguns, gives more flashes and faster recycling; for easier portability, a shoulder strap is provided. Some units are rechargeable. The more powerful flashguns offer a choice of power source – battery, power pack or main supply.

▲ **A slave unit** allows you to fire several flashguns at once. It reacts photoelectrically to the main flash, and activates the subsidiary flashgun it is linked to.

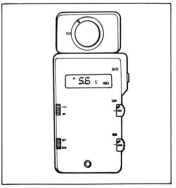

▲ **A flash meter** is a professional tool for incident-light readings of flash, accurate to within 1/3 stop, or even 1/10 stop. An LCD or LED display gives an instant readout.

LIGHTING FOR THE STUDIO

Tungsten lighting has special attractions for beginners. Its continuous illumination makes it easier to position lamps accurately, you can use a TTL or handheld meter to measure exposure, you do not have to wait for recycling, and you can set a slower shutter speed to blur movement. One drawback is that bulbs can get very hot. Studio flash units are more expensive. However, they offer greater power and versatility and can be used with daylight film without the need for corrective filtration.

● **Tungsten bulbs** are available in two main types: photolamps (or photofloods), the cheapest of which last for 3 to 6 hours and get redder and dimmer with use; and tungsten-halogen lamps, which are smaller and more expensive, last much longer and produce light of a constant color temperature.

● **Spotlights** use a Fresnel lens to produce a sharp, narrow beam. Some have a beam angle that can be varied between 40° and 80° at the turn of a knob.

● **Floodlights** provide softer light over a broad area. The more powerful ones have a fan to dissipate heat.

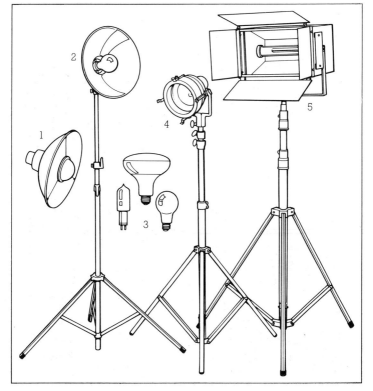

1. Photolamp with shallow bowl reflector and spiller cap to block direct light
2. Budget photolamp with standard alloy reflector
3. Selection of tungsten bulbs
4. Variable-beam spotlight (800 watts)
5. High-power floodlight (2,000 watts) with barndoors

● **Dichroic filters,** of heatproof glass, fit over some tungsten lights to convert them to daylight film.

● **Studio flash units** run off the main supply. They incorporate a tungsten modeling light, so that you can preview effects.

● **Flash power** is measured in joules or watt-seconds. The smallest studio units are rated at about 100 joules.

● **Budget studio flash units** combine flash tube, modeling light and power pack in one shell.

● **A Quad pack,** used with one or more larger flash units, is the heart of a typical professional setup. Up to four packs can be linked together to increase output. The pack offers less than two-second recycling.

● **Attachments** are available for studio lights to restrict, direct or diffuse the beam. To spread and soften the light, you can use a white or silver umbrella or, for greater diffusion, a window of translucent plastic. A snoot concentrates the beam. Barndoors control light spillage.

● **The most versatile supports** for lighting are telescopic stands. Also useful are clamps, and boom arms for overhead lighting.

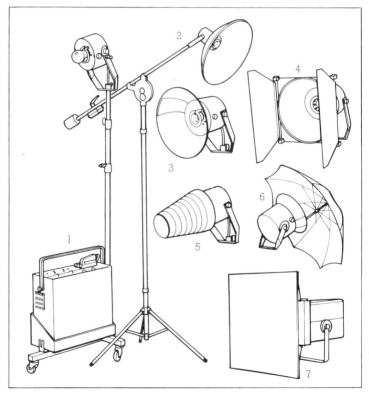

1. Quad power pack with 2,000 flash head
2. Unit with Softlite reflector (75° lighting angle) on boom arm
3. Keylite reflector (50°)
4. Barndoor with Keylite
5. Snoot
6. Paralite white umbrella
7. Budget Bo-lite flash unit with window attachment

THE TEMPORARY STUDIO

Few homes are without a room that can double as a studio. Work out a time-sharing arrangement within a living room, playroom, bedroom or garage. Use a separate room for dressing and makeup, or use screens for privacy.

● **Ordinary curtains** or blinds will darken the room sufficiently for photography with flash. With tungsten lights, put up heavy dark curtains.

● **To save space,** use spring clamps or screw clamps to support lighting. Use pads to safeguard paintwork.

● **Special wiring** is usually needed for tungsten lights exceeding three kilowatts in total.

1. Decorative wall mirror (useful as a prop)
2. Desk lamp for previewing lighting when using flash
3. Tea trolley on castors used for camera equipment and film
4. Cheval mirror, for fill-in lighting (and for checking hair and makeup)
5. Home-made reflector (white polystyrene on timber stand)
6. Tungsten lights on stands

7. Fan heater for warm or cool air (especially important for nude photography)
8. Roll of thick tracing paper to diffuse daylight (detaches from brackets when not in use)
9. Home-made stand for paper backgrounds
10. Various backgrounds and reflectors
11. White walls and ceiling (to avoid color casts)

THE PERMANENT STUDIO

● **A permanent studio** should be at least half as wide as it is long, with a special area for dressing and makeup. The minimum space you need to frame a full-length figure with an 85mm lens is 20 feet (6.2m).

● **The ceiling** should be 9 to 12 feet (2.7–3.7m) high – high enough to allow overhead lights, low enough for bouncing light.

● **Wooden shutters** are best for excluding light: you can lean large flat items against them if wall space is limited.

● **Good ventilation** is essential, especially with tungsten lights.

● **A smooth wooden floor,** unlike a carpet, allows you to walk over background paper without creasing it.

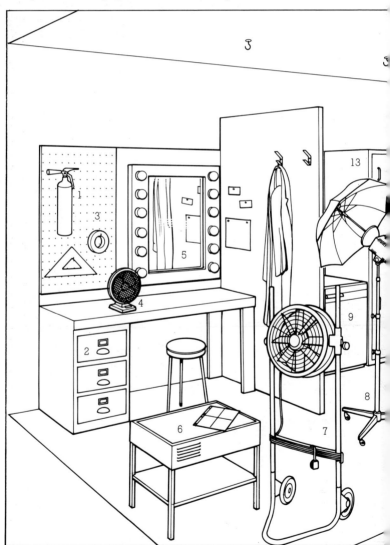

1. Fire extinguisher
2. Drawers for set-building tools
3. Pegboard
4. Small fan
5. Dressing area
6. Light box
7. Wind machine
8. Studio flash units with umbrellas
9. Refrigerator for storing film
10. Mirrors, reflectors and diffusers
11. Folding screen
12. Medium-format camera on tripod
13. Props cupboard
14. Colorama background paper in timber rack
15. Telescopic stand for background paper
16. Step ladder
17. Equipment trolley mounted on wheels
18. Hooks in ceiling for hanging backgrounds and lights

MASTERING BASIC SKILLS

Your camera outfit is more than just a means to create wholly sharp, correctly exposed images: you can also use it to *interpret* a picture, to create something more than a literal record of what the eye sees. To take full advantage of your equipment, you need to understand how a slight adjustment of aperture setting or shutter speed can produce a totally different image, even if the overall exposure remains the same. And you must also learn how to use and control the varying qualities of natural or artificial light, which in turn requires a knowledge of how different film types respond to varying levels of contrast in a subject.

● **Get to know your camera,**
until using its controls becomes
second nature. It may help, at first,
if you note down aperture and
shutter speed settings for all your
pictures. Confident camera-
handling will give you time to
concentrate on other aspects of
photography. Fumbling, on the
other hand, will usually make both
you and the model ill at ease.

● **Light** is often the key to a
successful picture. Study the way
light reveals and enhances
surfaces, and shadows conceal
parts of a scene to create
atmosphere and mystery. Explore
the changing pattern of highlights
and shadows in your pictures as
you vary viewpoint, pose and
exposure. Learn how to soften
light by diffusion or reflection.

USING TELEPHOTO LENSES

A standard lens records a scene in approximately the same perspective as the eye does, and is thus very useful for images in which the model appears in natural scale with her surroundings. However, for head-and-shoulders portraits a standard lens will tend to make the nose look too large and the ears too small. By choosing a short or medium telephoto lens for close-ups, you can remedy this problem, and at the same time subdue the background to a blur or compress the perspective of the scene to make distant features of the landscape appear nearer.

● **Generous framing** with a long lens may make it easier for the model to behave spontaneously. If your viewpoint is out of earshot, give her general posing guidelines before shooting, and encourage her to improvise.

● **In dim light,** the relatively small maximum apertures of telephoto lenses may cause problems. Make sure you pack some fast film, just in case.

● **Camera shake** is exaggerated with long lenses. Use a steady tripod. Or if you handhold, set a minimum shutter speed corresponding roughly to the focal length; for example, with a 105mm lens, set at least 1/125.

● **Against the sun,** choose a fixed lens in preference to a zoom, which is more likely to cause flare.

● **Haze** is exaggerated by long-focus lenses: use a skylight filter.

◀ A standard 55mm lens was ideal for conjuring up a pastoral idyll (left). To use the same lens for a close-up portrait, I could have avoided distorting the face by allowing some space around the model and enlarging just the central portion of the image during printing. But it would have been preferable to change to a longer lens, such as the 90mm lens used for the studio shot at the top of the page. Another approach is to use a standard lens with a 2× teleconverter.

▲ The shallow depth of field of a telephoto lens, combined with its compression of perspective, can sometimes create a powerful 3D effect, as in this lakeside portrait, taken with a 200mm lens. Because I wanted to catch the girl's fleeting gestures and expressions, I set a shutter speed of 1/250. This allowed me to handhold the camera, but prohibited me from setting the lens's widest aperture – f/3.5. However, the surface of the lake is sufficiently blurred at f/8 to isolate the model dramatically.

USING WIDE-ANGLE LENSES

Although unsuitable for flattering close-ups, medium wide-angle lenses (24mm to 35mm) have many advantages for the glamor photographer. They have good definition, relatively large maximum apertures, and can be handheld successfully even at shutter speeds down to 1/30. With careful choice of viewpoint and composition, you can encompass a broad view of the model's surroundings without obtrusive distortions. Or alternatively, you can exaggerate the way these lenses dramatize perspective to create special-effect images in which the model is bizarrely out of proportion, the foreground greatly enlarged, or straight lines within the scene made to converge to a vanishing point. With lenses shorter than 24mm, such deviations from the norm become even more spectacular; but, if you wish, you can still keep the model herself naturally proportioned, provided that she is not too near the camera, and that you choose the composition with care.

● **In a full-length view** taken with a wide-angle lens, you can prevent the model from appearing oddly proportioned by making sure that her head and limbs are all at equal distances from the camera. This may be easiest with a reclining pose.

● **Striking perspective effects** are obtainable by tilting the camera from a high or low viewpoint.

● **Barrel distortion,** affecting the edges of the image, may be conspicuous with lenses shorter than 28mm. To solve the problem, avoid placing straight lines, regular shapes or the model herself at the frame edges. Whereas a face or a round clock might be unacceptably distorted, foliage or ruffled fabrics would appear quite natural.

◄ Even a moderate wide-angle lens can be used for dramatic effects, provided that you make a bold choice of viewpoint and composition. I took the top image, opposite, with the camera tilted from a position close to floor level. Extreme wide-angle lenses offer even more possibilities for experiment. In the seaside image (left), taken with an 18mm lens, exaggerated perspective makes the figure weirdly distorted.

▲ With wide-angle lenses, there is often a danger that background details will appear indistinguishably tiny, or that the composition will be unbalanced by too much sky. One solution is to throw the emphasis onto the foreground by tilting the camera or choosing a viewpoint close to the ground. Above, I took the first of these approaches, which you could also apply to a field of flowers or boulders on a beach.

JUDGING EXPOSURE

Exposure meters are designed to average out the dark and light areas in the subject, and indicate an exposure that will be acceptable overall. A meter cannot identify the skin tones, often the most important part of a glamor image or nude study. Nor can a meter make creative choices about exposure – when to underexpose to intensify the mood, when to overexpose to soften the colors. You must therefore learn to judge the distribution of light in the scene, and overrule the meter's recommendation if necessary to obtain the desired effect.

● **Through-the-lens meters** usually measure the central portion of the viewfinder image. They also tend to be biased toward the bottom half of the frame to avoid readings being influenced by the sky. However, some TTL meters read from a small 'spot' in the center. Consult your camera manual, which may have a diagram to show the meter's precise field of coverage.

● **Slide film** is less tolerant of under- or overexposure than black-and-white or color print film. Fast films are more tolerant than slow films.

● **A bright background** (such as a blue sky) or a background that is light in tone (such as a white wall)

will deceive the meter into indicating too little exposure: give one or two stops extra.

● **A dark background** will yield an overexposed image if you follow the meter reading; give one or two stops less exposure than shown.

● **Bracket** to be sure of getting at least one acceptably exposed image. That is, take several frames of the same subject at different settings above and below the exposure you judge correct.

● **When exposure is tricky** to judge (for example, when bright sun causes high contrast), use one of the special metering techniques illustrated below:

▲ **Reading from the face.** Move the camera close to the face, or whatever area of the subject is most important. Set the exposure indicated by the TTL meter, then return to the chosen camera position to take the picture.

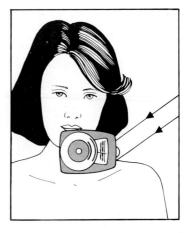

▲ **Incident light reading.** Use a handheld meter to take a reading of light falling onto the subject. Attach the meter's diffusing dome and, at the subject position, point the meter back toward the camera to take a reading.

▲ Bright highlights in this scene, taken in noonday sun, misled the TTL meter into producing an underexposed slide when the camera was set in the automatic mode. (Ektachrome 64, 1/60, f/16)

▲ In this frame on the same film, using the automatic mode with the exposure compensation dial set at +2 yielded an acceptably exposed background, with slightly burned-out skin tones. (1/15, f/16)

▲ A low-key image based on a close-up meter reading from the model's arm revealed skin texture and bodily form. Underexposure has saturated the colors of the glass and the rug. (1/250, f/16)

▲ Setting the exposure compensation dial to +3 has created a high-key image with softened colors and burned-out highlights. The lack of shadows suppresses modeling. (1/8, f/16)

HIGH KEY, LOW KEY

By overexposing a predominantly light-toned (that is, 'high-key') subject, you can reinforce a mood of cool artifice, and give flesh tones a pallid, fragile beauty. The opposite strategy is to underexpose to create a 'low-key' image – one whose tones are mainly dark. Because we are more familiar with dark-toned scenes in daily life, low-key images tend to look more natural. Although varying widely in mood from luxurious sensuality to romantic innocence, they almost always have an intimate quality, drawing us into a close relationship with the model – even when her gaze is not directed toward the camera.

● **For a high-key image,** the lighting should be flat and diffused. Outdoors, an overcast sky is usually best. Slight overexposure softens colors to produce a pastel effect. More extreme overexposure can make outlines disappear as they merge into a background of similar tone. Meter readings tend to reduce the brightness of a high-key subject, so you must usually give one or two stops extra.

● **For a low-key image,** the lighting should be contrasty, with patches of highlight that prevent the picture from looking merely somber. Sidelighting or back-lighting from direct sunlight or a small studio lamp are ideal. The usual approach is to judge exposure from the highlights: take an incident light reading, and use this as a basis for bracketing your pictures.

● **Slightly underexposing** a subject will give richer, denser colors and a more differentiated range of highlights. For this reason, many photographers choose to underexpose slide film by $\frac{1}{3}$ or $\frac{1}{2}$ stop even when there is a normal range of tones or brightness levels in the scene.

▲ Radical overexposure can make a model merge into her background, as in this image taken under a bright, cloudy sky. Four stops extra exposure bleached the green foliage. The lipstick, though, retains more color, and serves as a focal point.

▶ A cream dress is a high-key subject, but this girl's raven hair suggested a low-key approach. How much less dramatic the picture would have been if the model were blonde! Under-exposure isolated the face, and enriched skin tones.

► Slightly exaggerating the highlights in a low-key picture can often be a rewarding approach, as in the nude study, right. Here, a small, undiffused tungsten photolamp provided strongly directional lighting. I wanted the mood to be coldly mysterious, not cosily romantic. I therefore took an incident light reading and added one stop to the exposure indicated. This burned out highlight detail, so that the nude almost seems sculpted out of light itself. Slight overexposure also restored some detail to the shadowy background.

CAPTURING MOVEMENT

Although some glamor pictures are deliberately static, in others movement is a vital ingredient. In such cases, the photographer must make a creative choice: whether to freeze the action by selecting a fast shutter speed (or by electronic flash) or allow the movement to record as an expressive blur. Just how much blur there will be depends on the speed of movement, its direction in relation to the camera, and the size of the subject in relation to the total picture area.

● **Focusing is critical** when you photograph a model in motion. A fast shutter speed demands a wide aperture, which reduces depth of field. It is often helpful to prefocus on a fixed point before the model reaches it. You can use this approach if she is jumping off a wall or branch, or moving back and forth on a swing or seesaw.

● **A jogging figure** in the middle distance moving diagonally across your field can be frozen sharp at 1/125. If she is coming straight toward you, you can halve the speed. If she is running from side to side across the frame, quadruple it. A model more dominant in the frame requires a faster setting.

● **Frame a moving subject** generously: you may need to improve the composition afterward by cropping.

● **Electronic flash** freezes the fastest action; to combine a sharp image with a blurred trail, use flash in available light and set a shutter speed significantly slower than the camera's X setting.

▲ A motordrive is capable of capturing action in a rapid succession of frames. Use one to record a sequence of vigorous movements (as above and below) or fleeting expressions.

▲ For this image, I stopped down to extend depth of field. However, fast slide film allowed 1/125, freezing the model's gentle run.

▼ Splashing water always adds excitement to a picture. Here, a shutter speed of 1/60 blurred the splashes only slightly.

FOCUSING SELECTIVELY

Some nude and glamor pictures rely on overall sharpness for their impact. However, you can sometimes improve a composition by keeping selected areas deliberately blurred to concentrate the viewer's interest elsewhere within the picture frame. Thrown out of focus, colors are toned down and shapes become less obtrusive. You can use this effect to subdue a distracting background or foreground that would otherwise compete for attention with the model. Applying this technique successfully demands careful choice of lens, viewpoint and aperture to limit depth of field.

● **Use a long-focus lens** (at least 100mm) at a wide aperture to reduce depth of field in full-length views. With a normal or portrait lens, set the widest aperture and choose a closer viewpoint.

● **The viewfinder image** in an SLR camera shows the effect of opening up the lens to maximum. If you set a smaller than maximum aperture, use the lens's depth of field scale. Alternatively, use the camera's depth of field preview mechanism if it has one; this stops down the lens to the chosen setting and allows you to see what parts of the scene will appear out of focus.

(With K bayonet lenses, some photographers preview depth of field by releasing the lens catch and then twisting the lens slightly in its mount; however, this incurs a risk of dropping the lens.)

● **If the light is too bright** to allow a wide-open aperture, place the subject in shade or use a neutral density filter over the lens of the camera.

● **Slight blur** can sometimes look like a mistake. If you cannot make the blur more extreme, it might be preferable to keep the whole scene in sharp focus.

▲ Throwing the model herself out of focus is an unconventional approach that tends to work best when the composition is simple, as in this humorous juxtaposition of youth and age. I used a 50mm lens and set an aperture of f/2.8 to blur the nude in the foreground. This allowed a fast shutter speed, which froze the movement of the hens.

▶ A 135mm lens set at f/3.5 isolated the girl in pink between an out-of-focus background and foreground. Telephoto lenses require extra exposure to compensate for light being lost as it travels from lens to film; this makes it feasible to set a wide aperture, even in relatively bright conditions.

◀ A 2× teleconverter with a 50mm lens gave me an effective focal length of 100mm for this casual head-and-shoulders portrait. I set the lens to its widest aperture, f/2.8, so there was no need to use the camera's depth of field preview button. I could see from the viewfinder that the back-ground – a public park – would be blurred to an abstract pattern.

BALANCING COLOR

All color films are matched to a specific 'color temperature' – an index of the redness or blueness of a natural or artificial light source, quoted in kelvins. Although color temperature changes may be unnoticeable to the eye, substantial deviations can cause unwanted color casts on film. To ensure accurate color rendition, follow the filter recommendations given in the chart below, which shows the kelvin ratings for a range of light sources.

● **Daylight slide film** is matched to 5,500k – the color temperature of midday sunlight or flash. A cold blue cast will occur if the light has a higher color temperature (for example, in summer shade). A reddish cast will occur if the kelvin rating is lower (for example, in late-afternoon sun).

● **Tungsten slide film** is usually matched to 3,200k (Type B). An 81A filter will remove a bluish cast when using Type B film with photolamps, while an 82 series filter will correct for household lights. Special filtration may be needed when bulbs age or the voltage drops.

Light source	Color temperature Kelvins	Filtration with daylight balanced film	Filtration with tungsten (type B) film
Blue sky	20,000	85B	
	15,000	85	
	10,000	85C	
Hazy sunlight	9,000		
Average in shade, summer	8,000	81EF	
Overcast sky	7,000	81C	
Lightly overcast sky	6,500	81B	
	6,000	81A 81	
Summer sunlight/flash	5,500	NO FILTER 82	85B
	5,000	82A	85
Early morning and late afternoon sunlight	4,500	82B 82C 80D	85C
	4,000	80C	81EF 81C
1hr after sunrise/before sunset	3,500		81B
Photoflood bulb	3,400	80B	81A
	3,300		81
Tungsten halogen lamp	3,200	80A	NO FILTER
	3,100		82
	3,000		82A
100 watt light bulb	2,900		82B
	2,800		82C
40 watt light bulb	2,700		80D

● **Color conversion filters** make larger adjustments. The 80 strong blue series converts daylight film to tungsten light. The 85 strong amber series converts tungsten film for daylight.

● **A color meter** can be used for exact measurements of color temperature, but if this is beyond your price range and you have to guess the filtration, err on the warm side.

▲ Color casts are especially noticeable on skin tones, which we always subject to close scrutiny. For the picture above, I loaded Ektachrome 160 tungsten slide film. Because the color temperature of my studio lighting scheme was too low to yield correct colors, I fitted an 82 filter over the lens.

▲ An 81B filter, which requires an exposure increase of $\frac{1}{3}$ stop, is a good all-round choice for removing a bluish tinge from daylight slide film on overcast days or in open shade. I used one for the location shot, above, right. Because Ektachrome daylight film can sometimes give bluish results even in direct sunlight, some photographers use this film with an 81A filter permanently in place.

▶ The warm light of early morning or late afternoon can be flattering with some subjects. Although an 82C filter would have restored normal color to this photograph (right), such an adjustment would have detracted from the mood of the image, which owes everything to the golden hues.

USING DAYLIGHT

The quality of natural light changes according to the angle of the sun and the vagaries of weather. By learning how these variables affect the appearance of a photograph, and how you can influence the result by careful selection of exposure and viewpoint, you can harness daylight, indoors or out, to produce fresh-looking, flattering images.

● **Harsh, noonday sun** throws ugly shadows under the nose and chin. A solution is to position the model in an open, shady spot.

● **An overcast sky** or hazy sun softens shadows, reduces contrast and flatters the subject, though without obscuring modeling. Under gray skies, warm up the light with an 81 series filter.

● **Raking sunlight** early in the morning or late in the afternoon casts long, soft-edged shadows and reveals texture. Contrast is not extreme. Golden late-afternoon light is excellent for romantic mood pictures.

● **Against-the-light pictures** are always appealing. Use reflectors to fill in shadows. To prevent flare, keep the sun out of view, and use a lens hood. Look for rimlighting effects, when low sunlight edges your subject with a halo of light.

● **Indoors,** windows provide strongly directional lighting. A north-facing window gives consistently soft light. In direct sun, reflections from white walls may reduce contrast to an acceptable level. Otherwise, you can lower contrast by diffusion or reflection (as described overleaf); or exploit high contrast creatively for patterns of light and shade.

◄ The location for all three pictures here was a large indoor swimming pool on a cloudless autumn day. In the top image, opposite, direct light from a window to the left was supplemented by diffused light from behind the camera, which filled in the shadows. In the lower picture, I placed the model away from direct sunlight for a softer effect. Reflected highlights off the water added compositional interest.

▲ Inexperienced photographers sometimes find it surprising that bright sunlight can provide ideal conditions for a low-key effect, as in the picture above. Here, light streaming directly onto the model extended the brightness range of the scene to something like six stops. By following an incident light reading, I ensured that the highlights would be correctly exposed, while the shadows would lose detail. The result is a picture full of atmosphere.

CONTROLLING DAYLIGHT

Many amateur photographers treat sunlight as if it were totally beyond their control, and neglect to avail themselves of the various ways in which it can be manipulated. Perhaps this is because the sun is such an unimaginably remote light source. In fact, it is relatively easy to channel sunlight into the shadow areas of a scene, or to soften the light by diffusion. To apply these techniques, you can use readily available, inexpensive materials, as described below; many of these are items that can be found in any household. Usually, your aim should be to create a natural effect – as if the quality of light you wanted just happened to be there.

● **Contrast** that looks acceptable to the eye will often appear unacceptable on film – especially slow slide film, which has the narrowest brightness range. When photographing indoors near a window, or outdoors in direct sunlight, ask yourself whether you need to take special measures to retain shadow detail.

● **Use a white reflector** to fill in shadows. A white sheet hung on a wall is perfectly adequate. But more convenient is a large sheet of expanded polystyrene, available from building suppliers; this is lightweight and rigid, and can easily be leaned against a chair or natural feature. An open book or a newspaper will suffice in an emergency. Do not neglect reflectors in the landscape – for example, a whitewashed wall or a stretch of pale sand.

● **For brighter reflections,** use a silvery reflector – for example, kitchen foil taped to cardboard or polystyrene.

● **Screen light** from selected areas of a scene by using baffles of black paper or cardboard. This allows you to strengthen a composition by keeping unwanted detail in shadow.

● **Use spring clips** or gaffer tape to secure reflectors, baffles or screens in awkward places.

● **Light from a window** can be softened by placing diffusing material over it. Hang net curtains or other gauzy fabric over the window, or tape several thicknesses of artists' tracing paper over it. If you want to include the window in the picture, tape tracing paper to the *outside*.

◄ A wardrobe mirror provided effective fill-in lighting in this picture, and balanced the composition by duplicating the burned-out highlight area. When the mirror itself is not included in an image, you can reduce the intensity of reflected light by stretching one or more layers of mesh over its surface. A creative use of smaller mirrors is to introduce isolated highlight areas into a low-key picture.

▲ The size of a reflector, and its distance from the model, are both critical when filling in shadows. For this portrait, I used a three-feet-square sheet of polystyrene placed about a yard away. Moving the sheet further to the right, or using a smaller reflector such as an open book, would have darkened the shadows and divided the face unpleasingly into more extreme areas of light and dark.

MIXED LIGHTING

When a scene is illuminated by a mixture of daylight and artificial lighting, you are faced with a dilemma – which type of film should you load? Tungsten-balanced film will cause a cold blue cast in daylit areas, whereas daylight film will impart an orange glow to artificial lighting. Fitting a filter over the lens to correct for one type of illumination will create a color cast in the other type. Some possible ways to balance the color temperature, in order to remove unwanted color casts, are described below. However, it is often more productive to leave the imbalance undisturbed, and choose the film type according to whether you want to add warm, romantic touches to your picture, or a chilly twilight effect.

● **Daylight from a window** can be matched to tungsten film if you cover the window with orange transparent plastic the same color as an 85B filter; this is available from companies that supply movie-making equipment.

● **To avoid an orange cast** on daylight film, replace household bulbs by blue-tinted 'daylight' bulbs. Alternatively, use bounced flash to overwhelm the tungsten lighting.

● **To match photolamps** to daylight, fit heat-resistant glass filters over them. If you use a gelatin sheet, take care not to place it too close to the bulb, or overheating will occur.

▼ The main light source for this soft-focus picture of embracing nudes was a diffused photoflood. Tungsten film recorded the interior in natural hues, but caused the daylight scene beyond the window to look bluer.

▼ Table lamps, or oil lamps, provide isolated pools of light that always look attractive on daylight film. Here, I used bounced flash to fill in shadows opposite the window, which is just visible at the extreme left-hand side of the picture frame.

▲ A tungsten spotlight illuminated this nude and threw an oblique shadow on the grass. Tungsten film gave an accurate rendition of the skin tones. But because the house lights are lower in color temperature, they have a slightly orange tinge.

USING FLASH

Today's automatic portable flash units take the tedious arithmetic out of exposure judgments, while still offering scope for creative control. Because flash is a small, hard light source, it needs to be used sensitively to avoid unnatural-looking pictures. Experiment with all three techniques for softening the light illustrated below and on the opposite page.

● **'Red eye'** occurs when light from a flash unit shines directly into the eye and reflects back from blood vessels. Avoid it by moving the light off the lens axis or by diffusing the flash. Or with direct, on-camera flash, ask the model to look at a bright light just before you take the picture; as the pupils contract, red eye becomes less obtrusive.

● **Automatic flash units,** unlike manual units, usually offer a choice of aperture settings. Select the aperture according to the distance range and the depth of field required.

● **Check the output** of a new flash unit by performing exposure tests, trying out different aperture settings for a range of flash-subject distances.

● **Multiple flash** allows you to create soft, even lighting or illuminate a spacious interior. To synchronize two or more units, use either a multiple flash connector or, more conveniently, a slave cell attached to each additional unit. If the beams do not overlap, judge the exposure from the unit supplying the main lighting. If they do overlap, reduce exposure by up to one stop.

Direct flash mounted on the camera's hotshoe produces harsh and generally unflattering shadows. This approach is best avoided in nude and glamor photography, except for occasional special effects.

Diffused flash softens the light. Use a diffusing accessory or place white cloth or a handkerchief over the flash head. With a manual unit, you will need to give extra exposure; allow about one to two stops.

● **Use flash to freeze** fast movement. With an automatic unit, set the widest aperture so that the unit operates at low power, giving a briefer flash. This may make the background darker – an effect you can often use creatively to isolate the model from her surroundings.

● **Flash in daylight** (that is 'fill-in flash') is excellent for filling in harsh shadows, or putting highlights into the eyes in dull weather. When using fill-in lighting, you must ensure that the daylight remains dominant. Set the exposure for daylight and reduce flash power. Some automatic units have a half-power setting, but with most you need to set the unit's ISO control to twice your film speed. With a manual unit, do likewise, or place a double-thickness white handkerchief over the flash to reduce the output.

▲ For this fill-in flash image, I used a pale yellow filter over the flash to warm up the skin tones.

Off-camera flash makes shadows fall obliquely and accentuates texture. Link the unit to the camera by a sync lead. With portable flash, either mount the unit on a special camera bracket or hold it in your hand.

Bounced flash is best for soft, shadowless light. Use a white ceiling or white cardboard or polystyrene. With an automatic unit, aim the sensor toward the model, not the ceiling, or the picture will be underexposed.

STUDIO LIGHTING 1

The basis for a studio glamor photograph, whether a close-up or a half- or full-length portrait, should normally be a single main light source. Two lights of equal strength would produce shadows in conflicting directions, and the result would look perplexing and unreal. The classic arrangement is a directional 'key' lamp supplemented by a reflector, or a diffused floodlight, to lighten shadows without eliminating them entirely. Unless you are aiming for an intentionally harsh effect, you should usually soften the key light either by bouncing the beam off a reflective surface or by passing it through a translucent diffusing screen.

● **Tungsten lamps** in a darkened room allow you to see the effect of a scheme as the camera will see it. Build a dimmer switch into the circuit, so that you can reduce the output of the lights while you compose and focus; this prolongs the life of the bulbs.

● **Flash units** can be positioned more accurately if you use a reading lamp initially to work out the lighting angle. Studio flash units have a built-in tungsten modelling lamp for this purpose.

● **The standard position** for the main light is at approximately 45° to the subject. Placing the light more frontally reveals more detail in the face or figure but produces a flatter effect, with reduced modeling. Sidelighting obscures detail but creates a moodier, low-key image.

● **A larger reflector,** or one placed closer to the model, will make the shadows softer and paler. When using foil, crumple it to avoid losing shadows altogether.

● **A white umbrella,** used with a flash unit, produces a softer, more diffused light than a silvered umbrella. The closer you move the flash along the umbrella's handle toward the fabric, the greater the spread of light.

● **A fill-in lamp,** used instead of a reflector, gives you more control over highlights and shadows. Position the lamp near the camera (not where you would normally place a reflector), or it will cast competing shadows. An alternative approach is to bounce a fill-in light onto a reflector opposite the main light. Fill-in lighting should always be dimmer than the main lighting. No exposure compensation is necessary.

● **The height of the key lamp** radically affects the appearance of the features. In the classic 'Hollywood' portrait, the light is angled down at 45° from about 3 feet (1 meter) above the head; this accentuates cheekbones and gives a narrower, more oval look to the face.

1. A studio key light to the right of the camera produced strong modeling but left half the face completely in shadow. Reflections of the flash in the eyes created attractive catchlights.

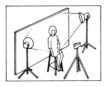

2. Adding a reflector on the shadow side gave more balanced lighting. An extra reflector on the model's knees would have filled in shadows under the chin.

3. Substituting a second light for the reflector, and setting it to half power, further lightened the shadow side and gave more shine to the hair.

▲ A diffused, frontal photolamp produced soft, flattering lighting and gave some color to the background. Modeling is limited, but a strong shadow defines the chin.

▲ Moving the diffused lamp further to the right models the features more distinctly, picks out highlights in the hair and faintly illuminates the background.

STUDIO LIGHTING 2

Although you should normally keep a lighting scheme as simple as possible, there are certain situations where additional lighting can make an important contribution. Set up the key lamp first and ensure that you are satisfied with its position and angle before introducing any supplementary lights.

● **Narrowing the beam** is often essential to prevent the supplementary light from spilling where it is not required. Use either a spotlight, or barndoors, a snoot or a honeycomb. You can easily make your own snoot with a cone of black cardboard, taped to the edge of the lamp's reflector. Similarly, you can improvise barndoors with two rectangular pieces of cardboard.

● **Add sparkle to hair** by directing a narrow beam onto it from a position behind the model. (See page 76.)

● **Lighting the background** separately removes shadows cast by the model and reveals background detail or texture. For even lighting, use two diffused lights aimed diagonally at different halves of the background, with the model placed just forward of the point where the beams cross. For a more atmospheric effect, use just one lamp to create a pool of light.

● **Use multiple lighting** for an extremely high-key, virtually shadowless effect. This is trickier than it sounds, especially with full-figure views. At least three lamps are needed: one or two broad, diffused frontal lights, plus extra lights on the background, perhaps bounced off a white ceiling. Restrict dark tones to a minimum: dark eyelashes or lipstick will stand out dramatically in a high-key picture if there are no other dark areas to compete with them. Follow an incident light reading. If there are no bright highlights, you can enhance the effect by overexposure.

▲ Two lamps lit the background of this portrait separately, over-whelming shadows that would otherwise have been cast by the off-camera key lamp.

▲ The multiple lighting for this picture was virtually identical to that used for the adjacent image. Here, though, I obtained a high-key effect by overexposure.

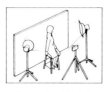

◀ Instead of lighting the Colorama background evenly for this somewhat petulant portrait, I used one spotlight angled obliquely from a position left of camera. This produced graduated color, and picked out shallow creases that show as an attractive mottled pattern.

▲ Multiple lighting schemes are useful for special effects. The setup for this image included a snooted lamp aimed at the backcloth to suggest a sunburst on a rainy day. It is fun to experiment with even more elaborate schemes. For example, try bottomlighting a nude: pose her on a glass platform covered with tracing paper, aim a lamp up from beneath, and use additional, diffused sidelighting to give soft modeling.

53

USING SHADOWS

In photographs where shadows are exploited for atmosphere or drama, lighting becomes a conspicuous element of composition, and may be almost as important as the model herself. You can use low-key lighting to mimic the intimacy of a dimly lit or shuttered room; or you can take a more extreme approach, creating fantasy pictures in which shadows form hard-edged, graphic shapes or contrast starkly with scorching highlights.

● **A low-key image** should have at least one small highlight area. Contrast will be greater than the exposure latitude of the film; you should therefore use reflectors to retain some detail in all but the darkest shadows. Judge exposure from the fully lit areas. Bracket generously, in half-stops.

● **In a light-toned room,** beware of reflections from walls, which may fill in shadows undesirably.

To prevent this, place black cardboard on the shadow side of the model.

● **A single spotlight** or snooted flood, aimed obliquely, will cast sharp elongated shadows and emphasize texture.

● **Silhouette the model** by bouncing light off a white background. Use a very weak fill light if you wish to retain some detail.

▲ For this silhouette, I angled two tungsten-halogen lamps onto the background and judged exposure from the highlights.

▲ Here, I used the same lighting setup, but with a small spot trained on the face, placed at a distance to soften its effect.

▲ A spotlight isolated this model's face from a surrounding area of high-contrast light and shade – an example of shadows being used with theatrical exaggeration rather than realistically.

◄ Another black-and-white image that owes its effect to judicious spotlighting. I placed the light above and behind the model to rimlight her profile. Available light filtering weakly into the room through a window obviated the need for a reflector. The broad exposure latitude of black-and-white film preserved plenty of shadow detail.

CHOOSING FILM

Most serious photographers use color slide or black-and-white film, choosing the 'speed', or sensitivity, according to the lighting conditions in which they plan to work and the image sharpness required. A drawback of color negative film is that, unless you process it yourself, you cannot readily underexpose or overexpose for effect: such decisions tend to be 'corrected' at the processing lab during printing.

● **Slow film** (such as Kodachrome 25 color slide film or Panatomic-X black-and-white film) has fine grain. It is the best choice when you want to record subtle detail or texture.

● **Medium-speed film** (ISO 50 to 100) is a good general-purpose film, suitable for moderate light levels when the subject is relatively static.

● **Fast film** is useful in weak light, and also allows you to set a narrow aperture to extend depth of field or a fast shutter speed to freeze motion. Although the image will be grainy, this can reinforce the mood.

● **Pushing** fast black-and-white film or color slide film enables you to cope with weaker light, although most glamor photographers use the technique to exaggerate grain. On the camera's ISO dial, set a film speed one, two or three stops higher than the film in use. Ask the lab to compensate by extra development.

● **Black-and-white film** is suitable for strong graphic images, as well as muted atmospheric effects. You can use black-and-white in daylight, flash or tungsten lighting without having to concern yourself with color temperature (see page 40). With an enlarger and a few other items of equipment, you can easily print your own black-and-white pictures, controlling the final appearance of the image.

▼ Print quality depends on the size of the negative and the enlargement as well as on film speed. The print below, enlarged from rollfilm, showed excellent detail, even though the film was medium-speed.

▼ Pushing a film to increase the effective film speed strengthens contrast, which can be useful on a dull day, when contrast is usually poor. The same technique softens colors, as in the portrait below, which was pushed two stops. For the low-key image (right) taken in a dark interior by available light, I pushed Ektachrome 400 film three stops, which compressed the density range to produce a stark composition.

▼ Kodachrome daylight-balanced 35mm slide films are notable for their bright, saturated hues, and accurate skin tones. They are available in two speeds – ISO 25 and 64. I used the former for the outdoor nude below. Slow films have a narrower exposure latitude than medium or fast films. Kodachrome 25, for example, has a tolerance of only half a stop either way, which makes accurate metering essential.

COMPOSING WITH COLOR 1

As a glamor photographer, you can often change background and clothes at will, and thus have a large measure of control over the color content of your images. Even on outdoor sessions, you can select background colors to a considerable extent according to your choice of viewpoint, lens and framing. To exercise this freedom successfully, you must be decisive about the mood you want to create – perhaps a feminine ambience with pastel shades, or a more aggressive feel with red background, dress or props, echoed by lipstick. If the model has an extrovert character, choose vivid, contrasting colors. Or for a more reflective effect, select a harmonizing scheme, with colors that are neighbors in the spectrum.

● **Limiting a picture** to just one or two harmonizing colors works particularly well if the scene contains strong shapes, subtle textures or a full range of tones. This is frequently the best approach with nudes, especially if you select warm colors.

● **Bright colors** appear more saturated if you take the exposure reading from the area in which the color appears. This will underexpose duller parts of the scene and enhance the chosen color by contrast. Saturation can also be increased by using a polarizing filter, or by underexposing slide film a half-stop.

● **Slow slide films** give better color saturation than fast films.

● **Warm color accents** against a background of predominantly cool hues create a dynamic effect.

● **Rain, mist and smoke** scatter the light and subdue colors, making clashing hues sit more comfortably together.

● **On location,** you can often restrict the color content of an image by using a telephoto lens.

▶ The colors that create the most effective color accents are the warm ones – reds, yellows and blazing oranges. This splash of yellow against turquoise immediately fixes our eyes upon the girl. Only when our interest is focused in this way do we notice the much smaller accent provided by the red flower in the girl's hair.

▶ In the location shot (near right), the dominance of yellow was artfully strengthened by a yellow wig. The studio picture (far right) owes its restfulness to subtle variations of green.

COMPOSING WITH COLOR 2

● **When balancing color areas,** bear in mind that different hues are perceived to have different strengths, or weights. Red looks heaviest, followed by orange, blue and green (all approximately equal), then yellow, then white.

● **Red** appears to advance forward from a picture. Just a small red patch will add vivacity to a photograph. Use larger areas with caution, or an unwanted color clash may occur.

● **Blue** appears to recede, suggesting distance, and thus makes a good background – especially if there are warm colors in the foreground.

● **Yellow** creates an optimistic mood, and is flattering to dark or suntanned skin. Slight underexposure will not make yellows look more saturated, as it

does with other hues; instead they will merely look muddier.

● **Green** is tranquil, with overtones of youthfulness and growth. UV radiation from a blue sky can sometimes make green leaves look too blue; to counteract this, use a skylight filter.

● **White** conveys virginal innocence. It is difficult to reproduce accurately on film, as it reflects the colors of its surroundings. You may need to use color compensating or light-balancing filters. When photographing a model in white or against a white background, avoid wearing colored clothing.

● **Black** makes other colors look brighter and more saturated by contrast. Conversely, an area of pale color or white will make a dense black seem richer.

▲ The gray wall of a farm building, with hints of yellow and green, provided the perfect foil for a bright splash of red. In the half-length portrait (above right), for which I used a polarizing filter, the red area is balanced against an equally saturated blue sky.

▶ The color scheme for this portrait is based on a combination found in nature – brown earth under a blue sky – which helps to account for the healthy, outdoor feeling. I chose the dress to match the extraordinary limpid blue of the model's eyes.

61

USING BLACK-AND-WHITE 1

Far from being the poor relation of color, black-and-white film offers a simplicity and clarity that color film seldom permits. To exploit the medium fruitfully, you need to re-educate your perceptions so that you can drain the world of color and see purely in tones. I would also recommend you to learn home developing and printing techniques. These enable you to control the detail and contrast in a picture according to your own imaginative interpretation of the subject.

● **Choose backgrounds** with care. A brilliant-hued background that would work in color might fail in monochrome if too similar in tone to skin or clothing.

● **Hard, contrasty lighting** is often best. Take meter readings of highlights and shadows; the difference in a portrait should be about 4 stops.

▶ Prints with significant areas of rich, velvety black often have impressive impact, as in the images opposite and below. You can strengthen this effect by dodging – that is, using a mask during printing to black out selected highlights or midtones. The lower picture opposite uses a shadow area to offset subtle tonal differences in the face.

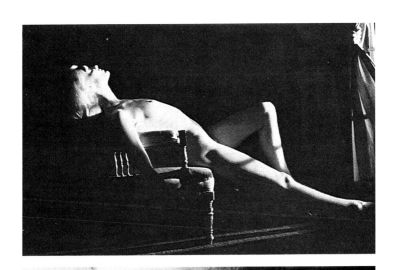

USING BLACK-AND-WHITE 2

● **Take light readings** to judge the similarity between tones. If two parts of a subject require equal exposure, they will appear virtually the same shade on a print.

● **Color filters** can be used to adjust the tones in a black-and-white picture. A blue filter prevents skin tones from looking too pale in tungsten light. Outdoors, a green filter adds an instant 'suntan'. An orange filter lightens skin and removes blemishes.

● **Use a UV filter,** not a skylight filter, to reduce haze; otherwise contrast will be weakened.

● **To reduce grain** using a 35mm camera, load a high-resolution film such as Kodak's Technical Pan or Panatomic-X.

● **To intensify grain,** push-process fast film and make a big

enlargement, or enlarge just a portion of the negative. Alternatively, sandwich a commercially produced 'grain screen' with the negative during printing.

● **Chromogenic films** (or dye-image films) are black-and-white negative films designed for processing in color negative chemicals. The final image is formed of dye, free of silver. The films have enormous exposure latitude. Generous exposure leads to ultrafine grain.

● **Choose a grade** of printing paper that will reinforce the impact. A hard paper increases contrast; a soft paper reduces contrast and shows more detail.

▼ Black-and-white film can have a unifying effect on composition. Both pictures on these two pages would have looked discordant in color.

CREATING AN IDEAL

The concept of glamor has come under attack in recent years. Its critics object to female stereotyping: why should women be expected to have unblemished skin, slim or curvaceous bodies, or lustrous hair? My answer to this line of argument is that you can glamorize a picture and still present a valid, *imaginative* view of the female face or form. To adapt reality to an ideal – an artistic ideal far removed from the degrading superficialities of the pin-up – stretches your lighting and camera-handling skills and requires an understanding of mood, color, composition and many other of the more subtle aspects of photography.

● **Exclude inessentials:** the simplest images are often the most glamorous. Even when you use a detailed context, such as a bedroom, make sure that all the details in the frame contribute something to the planned effect. You can often use shadows to exclude irrelevant detail, provided that you judge exposure with care.

● **Decide on the mood** you want to convey before planning a picture. The following adjectives may spark off ideas: exuberant, flirtatious, challenging, determined, amused, coy, guarded, pensive, romantic, wistful, somber, sultry, relaxed, langorous, preoccupied, enigmatic, classic, impersonal, austere, futuristic.

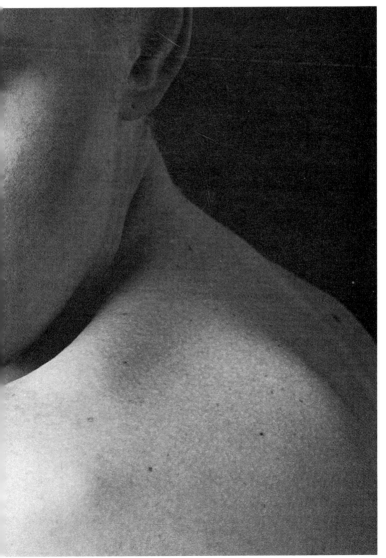

DIRECTING A MODEL

However well you know your model, developing a working rapport with her requires special skills. Any nervousness on her part, or indecision on yours, will be apparent in your photographs. Set up equipment, backgrounds and props beforehand, and make notes on the picture ideas you want to try. Consider the model's well-being, and give her regular breaks – at least hourly during a long session. Defuse any awkwardness by a friendly, open (but not over-familiar) manner. Convey your intentions by gentle encouragement rather than direct instruction. Compliments freely given will boost the model's confidence and lead to more spontaneous poses and expressions.

● **Work quickly,** and don't be too sparing with film. If you take pictures in rapid succession, the model does not have time to become tense before each new shot. To accelerate the pace, many professionals use a motordrive.

● **A tripod** lets you concentrate on directing the model, without having to spend too much time framing the image in the viewfinder.

● **Don't be pessimistic,** even if things go badly to start with; most models relax more as the session progresses.

● **Props** help to reassure a nervous model, especially if they give her something to do with her hands.

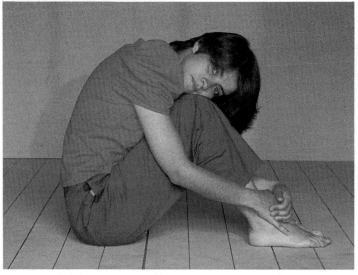

Complex lighting can intimidate an inexperienced model. For these casual portraits I used diffused afternoon light from a window behind the camera position. I knew that the simple setting and unostentatious clothes would draw attention to the poses, so it was important to keep the model relaxed by a steady flow of talk. As a thankyou for a photo session, it is always a good idea to offer the model a set of enlargements, as I did in this case.

CHOOSING THE POSE

A glamor pose should be pleasing purely as a composition, as well as being believable, as if the picture had evolved from a continuous flow of movement – as, indeed, it normally should. Turning the figure at 45° to the lens axis, or twisting just the torso, will flatter body curves. To add zest and a sense of dynamic movement to a picture, use poses based on diagonals. Try contrasting soft contours with sharply angled limbs.

● **The position of the hands** is crucial, even in full-length portraits. Awkwardly posed hands betray tension. When using a 50mm lens, avoid having the hands or feet too close to the camera, or they will appear too large.

● **Check the overall effect** in purely pictorial terms before releasing the shutter, ignoring expression. Ensure that all the body lines are graceful and fluid, and that each limb makes a positive contribution to the total effect.

◄ Shoulders tilted in relation to both the horizontal, and to the line of the head, are features of the two pictures on this page. Left, I offset the curving hip against the sharp angle of the left arm. By contrast, the pose below is based entirely on angles, while the pillow provides a counterpoint of curves.

▲ A successful pose does not
always have to look natural. Of the
four pictures here, only the top
one could pass for a moment from
daily life. The pose should never
conflict with, and may be designed
expressly to display, the model's
clothes. For example, the stance
above shows off a flowing dress.
By contrast, the shapely pose, left,
was suggested by a figure-
hugging leotard, while the silvery
jacket (above left) was suited to an
extrovert pose, thrusting forward
out of the picture.

HEAD-AND-SHOULDERS

Capturing expression and character in a head-and-shoulders portrait can be a challenge, as there are fewer poses available than with broader views. To avoid the stiff formality of a passport photo, you should vary the line of neck and shoulders. However, a symmetrical, full-face view can work if the model has strong features and can adopt an assertive expression.

● **The tilt of the head** is crucial in conveying personality. An upturned head suggests self-confidence, while a downward tilt suggests shyness or submission. Exaggerate these effects by lowering or raising the camera.

● **Profile views** show hair to advantage. Emphasize a fine profile by lifting the model's head to elongate the neck. Although women usually have firm views about which is their better side, feel free to disagree.

● **Bold framing** can improve a portrait. Do not be afraid to crop off the top of the head. When you frame close, a medium long-focus lens will prevent your inhibiting the model and distorting her features.

● **To slim a round face,** use a narrowed light source and ask the model to lower her head slightly. Conversely, you can widen a thin face by using a broadly diffused frontal light and a raised head.

▼ Over-the-shoulder glances are the staple diet of glamor. Here hunched shoulders and a low viewpoint create an arresting image, as well as disguising neck wrinkles – an effect you can also achieve with a scarf or high collar.

▶ A pensive portrait that is high-key (right) can be just as atmospheric as a low-key shot (above). Accessories, makeup, an exaggerated pose and viewpoint helped to create a Hollywood mood in the image below.

CLOTHES AND ACCESSORIES

After you have found your model, it makes sense to arrange a preview of her wardrobe. Individual garments or accessories may stimulate an original picture idea. Evening wear, lingerie and swimwear are obvious choices, but don't neglect humbler items such as voluminous old cardigans or even paint-spattered overalls! Try using the clothes in unconventional ways: disregard for convention can often reinforce the glamor.

● **Reveal the texture** of fabrics or furs with diffused, directional lighting. Backlighting can be a rewarding approach to diaphanous materials.

● **Capes, scarves and shawls** can be used to add a touch of dynamism to a glamor image. Ask the model to swirl or toss such accessories; freeze the action with electronic flash. Lace shawls look especially effective when photographed in black-and-white.

● **Keep a store of pins** and clothespegs handy. You can use these, hidden from the camera, to manipulate folds and gathers in loose garments.

◀ A simple garment dominates all three images on the opposite page. In the graphic sweatshirt image (top), I closed in to reduce the skin tones to a suggestive minimum. The shiny disco blouse (far left) was very photogenic: in this shot its crumpled texture is revealed by reflections of light from a window. A plastic trash bag might seem an odd choice of garment, yet the image at near left is challenging rather than comic, because of the sultry look I coaxed out of the model.

▲ Most thin fabrics become see-through when photographed against the light, revealing body shapes in silhouette. I used this technique for the exotic location photograph at the top of this page. Notice how the gold discs, catching the setting sun, add a suggestion of luxury to the image. If you want skin to show through the fabric, an effective method is to drench the garment in water, as in the other two pictures here (above and above left), both taken near an outdoor pool.

HAIR

Tossed with calculated abandon, hair can add movement to a picture, breathing into it a spirit of natural exuberance; plaited, beribboned, tied up or back, or otherwise manipulated, hair can also help to establish a mood of glamorous artifice. Knowing how to arrange the hair – the most pliable of all a model's attributes – is one of the basic skills of glamor photography. Just as important, however, is a knowledgeable approach to lighting: without this, even the most lustrous hair can look disappointing when you finally see the picture.

● **Backlighting** creates a halo that is especially effective with a full head of hair. In daylight, ensure the model is between the camera and the sun, and use reflectors to avoid throwing the face into shadow. A lens hood reduces the risk of flare.

● **A hair light,** added to the main lighting scheme, is a standard device in studio shots for adding brilliance to the hair or for separating hair from a background of similar color. Simply direct the narrow beam of a spotlight or snooted floodlight onto the hair from above and behind, or below and behind, the subject. Brunette hair requires brighter illumination than blond. Dull hair, whatever the color, demands quite intense lighting.

▲ Swirling hair, in the picture above, creates a vivid contrast with the face yet blends into the mossy background. Compare this with the very different image below, in which a plain studio background shows off long tresses.

● **Add body** to long hair or medium-length hair by asking the model to lower her head and then toss her hair vigorously back into place.

● **An electric fan** is useful in the studio to recreate the effect of a breeze lifting hair off the face. To simulate more boisterous winds, professional photographers sometimes use a wind machine.

● **Two models together** often look good if they have contrasting hairstyles. For example, you could try juxtaposing closely cropped raven-black hair with an unkempt cascade of blond.

● **Local hairdressers** can often provide useful help with styling. You may be able to obtain their services free, in return for pictures they can use for publicity displays.

▲ Gravity came to my aid for the portrait above, in which the hair streams as if in a hurricane. The model lay on her back (see diagram, right), lit by a floodlight bounced off the ceiling. I turned the resulting picture round from a vertical to a horizontal format to create the illusion. The picture below depends on a similar re-orientation: the girl lay on the floor, her hair spread around her. Turn the image sideways (hair at bottom) to see how it looked in the viewfinder.

MAKEUP

It is unwise to assume that an amateur model will be skilled in the art of makeup. By learning the rudiments of the craft yourself, you may be able to offer important guidance. The aim is usually to disguise blemishes, emphasize eyes, mouth and bone structure, and regularize the features by shading.

● **Use shading makeup** to balance the face, slim down a broad jaw or make a long nose seem shorter.

● **Use highlight makeup** to accentuate features. For example, a highlight down the ridge of the nose will lengthen the face.

● **Outline the lips** either just inside or outside their natural line to narrow or enlarge the mouth.

● **Overexpose** slightly to disguise the texture of makeup.

● **For flash-lit sessions,** make up under 'daylight' bulbs.

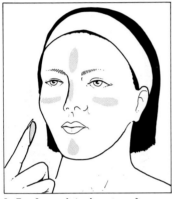

1. Apply moisturizer to soften skin. Apply foundation. Then paint out blemishes with concealer. To set the makeup, dust on translucent powder.

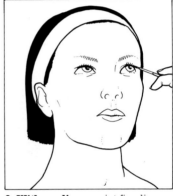

2. With eyeliner, paint fine lines along the lower eyelids. Then paint lines along the top lids to meet the lower lines, accentuating the corners.

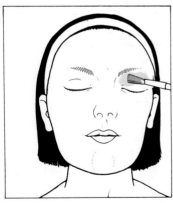

3. Brush eyeshadow lightly into the areas between the lashes and brows. Use a finger to soften the effect.

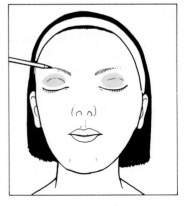

4. Define the eyebrows with a pencil. Take special care not to make the eyebrows too dark in relation to the hair color.

A basic makeup kit
1. Eyeliner
2. Eyeshadow for lids
3. Eyeshadow for sockets
4. Mascara/eyebrow brush
5. Eyebrow pencil
6. Highlight powder
7. Eye makeup brush
8. Blusher brush
9. Blusher
10. Foundation
11. Lip pencil
12. Lip brush
13. Mascara block and applicator
14. Lipstick

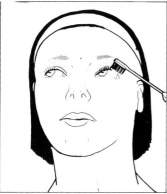

5. Apply mascara to the top and bottom lashes. But first take the precaution of powdering the lashes so that the mascara will not make them stick together.

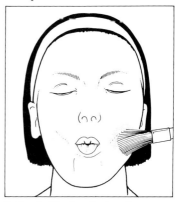

6. Apply blusher below the cheekbones with a soft brush to emphasize bone structure and add color to the face. Use sweeping, upward strokes.

7. Outline the mouth with a lip pencil or a fine brush. Use a shade slightly darker than that of the lipstick color.

8. Apply lipstick with a brush over the whole area of the lips. To give a natural shine, apply gloss over the lipstick.

EXPRESSIONS

Facial expression is usually crucial to the mood of a glamor portrait. To capture the look you want requires patience and understanding. The essential thing is to make the model feel relaxed and then try to get her in sympathy with your intentions. Showing her pictures in magazines or in your own portfolio can sometimes clarify the effect you are seeking but don't just ask her to copy a particular expression. Instead, try to generate the mood subtly, by talking and perhaps playing suitable music on a record or tape. Above all, don't expect a model to adapt expressions that don't come naturally.

● **To encourage laughter,** try recounting true anecdotes – not jokes, which may make the model feel uneasy, especially if she has heard them before.

● **Keep the model comfortable** – neither too hot nor too cool – or she will be unable to relax.

● **Coax a pensive look** by playing soft music. Tell a suitable story or describe a situation, and ask the model to concentrate on it.

● **Choose a pose** that complements the expression. For example, a provocative come-hither look is emphasized if the model looks back over her shoulder. A leaning pose is suitable for a dreamy, thoughtful expression.

▲ An expression need not always suggest an instantly identifiable state of mind. For example, it is impossible to tell whether this girl is looking alertly (perhaps anxiously?) out of the window, or whether she is lost in her own thoughts. Such ambiguities of mood can make a portrait more haunting.

▶ When you close in on the face, as in the picture opposite, it is essential to make sure that the model's whole body is relaxed: any tension or discomfort will show in the mouth and eyes. For the sequence below, I took a more vigorous approach, using jokes and clowning to encourage an extrovert performance.

USING PROPS

Props can improve a glamor picture in all manner of ways: they can give the model something to do with her hands, enlarge the range of possible poses, help balance the composition, add areas of harmonizing or contrasting color, suggest a scenario or evoke a mood. They can charge a photo with eroticism or add an intriguing touch of the surreal. Simple items that can be found in any home, such as hats, books, handmirrors, plants, telephones or umbrellas, are often the most effective. But you should also make a habit of collecting simple but unusual props and using them imaginatively and adventurously, whether indoors or on location.

● **Look out** for suitable objects when visiting friends; note them for future borrowing.

● **Hide parts of the face** or body with props to tantalize the viewer.

● **Allow the model** time to discover her own ways of using a prop effectively.

● **Keep paints and brushes** handy: if the color of the prop is wrong, you may be able to paint it. Alternatively, use black-and-white film.

▶ In nude studies, quite ordinary props can look effectively incongruous (right and below). Even in close-ups, a prop can make a contribution; for example, the exotic cigarette which draws attention to full lips.

▲ The brightly colored goggles would be obvious candidates for any props cupboard; they transform the image yet require a bare minimum of preparation.

▼ This studio shot shows an elaborate use of props, with globe lights, an unusual white cap and sheets of shiny plastic which produce distorted reflections.

FORMAT AND CROPPING

With slide film, you must make creative choices about framing at the picture-taking stage – whether to opt for a horizontal or vertical format, whether to close in on the model or allow plenty of space around her. Only when having prints made from the slides is there a chance to overturn these initial decisions. However, with print film you can suspend framing judgments until you see a contact sheet or proof print. You can then experiment with various crops (using masks as described below) until you find a composition that looks just right.

● **Format** affects the impact of a picture. A horizontally framed image often has a more tranquil feel than a vertical image. Choosing a format contrary to the way the model is oriented can produce a striking effect. For example, try framing a reclining model vertically, placing her high in the frame and using a wide-angle lens to increase the foreground area.

● **A square format,** such as that of $2\frac{1}{4} \times 2\frac{1}{4}$-inch (6 × 6-cm) rollfilm, sometimes makes a picture seem too static. To avoid this, choose asymmetrical compositions.

● **Use L-shaped masks** as an aid to making decisions about cropping when you examine a contact sheet or a proof print. Cut two masks out of a sheet of cardboard, place them over the proof to create a rectangular window, and then adjust their positions until you obtain the optimum framing. Mark the chosen crop carefully with a grease pencil and send the marked-up proof along with the negative when you order enlargements.

▲ This image was taken on $2\frac{1}{4} \times 2\frac{1}{4}$-inch rollfilm. To emphasize the juxtaposition of church and nude, I cropped to vertical format. A horizontal crop (below) concentrated on the bizarre contrast when two cows appeared on the scene.

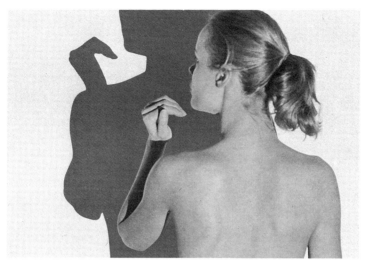

▲ Close framing added to the impact of this graphic shadow study, taken on Ektachrome 200 35mm slide film.

▼ A frame within the frame prevents this image on $2\frac{1}{4} \times 2\frac{1}{4}$-inch rollfilm from seeming too rigidly symmetrical.

85

USING FRAMES

The main use of a frame is to draw the eye towards the subject of a picture – in glamor photography, the model. However, a frame can also have various other functions: to obscure unwanted details, to impart a sense of depth, or to enliven an image by establishing a contrast of hue, tone, texture or scale. A good frame has saved many an unpromising location. Keep an eye open for framing possibilities whenever you size up a potential site. And remember, too, that you can sometimes introduce your own frame into a scene – for example, the rectangular outline of a deckchair in a backlit silhouette, a decorative mirror surround in a view showing the model's reflection, or the window of an open car door.

● **Exploit doorways and windows.** But in bright sunlight beware of exposure problems. It is usually preferable to photograph from outside looking in, as filled-in shadows in the background are more acceptable than burned-out highlights, and can simplify composition.

● **Blur a foreground frame** by selecting a wide aperture; this helps to draw attention to the model. Choosing a frame that is darker than the main subject has the same effect.

● **Use a frame to crop** part of the model from view. This can strengthen the composition, especially when a straight line cuts across body curves.

▲ The resemblance between an ornate mirror and a picture frame gave me the idea for this visual puzzle, in which the model looks like a photo. Below, I threw foliage out-of-focus to frame a portrait.

▼ To match the symmetrical geometry of this Indian archway, I chose a formal pose, positioning the model centrally. An upward-tilted camera made the sides of the arch converge.

▲ Elaborate frames that occupy a large proportion of the image can work well if the model remains the main focus of interest. Here, the face is highlighted against an area of dark shadow.

▼ The idea for this picture was based entirely on three props – the lipstick, the headscarf and the vintage Rolls Royce! A long lens allowed me to focus selectively, making the car less dominant.

CAMERA ANGLES

Choosing an unexpected camera angle is one of the simplest and most effective ways of investing a picture with drama. Try taking this approach at the end of a glamor session, when you are pleased with the images you have already captured on film and can now afford to experiment a little. The hardest lesson is not to be afraid of extremes: lack of conviction can spoil a potentially exciting image. To dramatize the effects of an upward-tilted or downward-tilted camera, you should use a wide-angle lens: a 28mm lens is an excellent choice, as the pictures on these two pages show. An extreme viewpoint not only creates unusual scale and perspective effects, but can also simplify the background.

● **A low viewpoint,** making the model seem to tower monumentally, usually demands careful attention to lighting to prevent ugly shadows from forming under the chin. In the picture on the opposite page, this problem is partially solved by the white dress, which acts like a reflector. In addition, I avoided black shadows by overexposing the image for a high-key effect.

● **A high viewpoint,** such as a window or balcony, can offer spectacular photographic opportunities, especially if you use foreground detail to establish a startling juxtaposition of scale, as in the dizzying picture below. Here, I left the foreground blurred to draw more attention to the nude and show the scene as the eye would see it, only partially in focus.

CANDID BEAUTY

Catching your subject unawares – or seemingly so – often yields pictures that are delightfully fresh and spontaneous, revealing personality far more than a formal portrait can. This approach is ideal for catching a carefree expression, or with girls who tend to become awkward or shy when asked to pose. Choose simple everyday settings and shoot in available light. Encourage your subject to act naturally – but only expect her to do so if you are equally unembarrassed about taking pictures. Never neglect golden opportunities such as weddings, seaside outings, picnics, parties or celebration meals.

● **Use a long lens** to avoid inhibiting your subject. Prefocus and preset the exposure. If the girl is likely to move around, stop down as much as the light allows.

● **An autofocus compact camera** is inconspicuous, and can be used for quickly 'snatched' images. The type with a quiet leaf shutter is less likely to be heard than the kind with a motorized wind-on.

▶ For the café view (right) I used a 135mm lens, setting a wide aperture to blur the background. The picture below shows a happy reunion: the girl was too overjoyed to worry about the presence of the camera.

▲ Shop windows provided the background for this early evening view, taken with a zoom lens set at about 150mm. I used fast slide film – Ektachrome 400 – to cope with the relatively dim light.

▼ A dressing table has strong connotations of privacy. This is why the picture below has such an intimate feel, which I stressed by using a lamp and mirror as a frame. I used fill-in flash.

GROUPS AND PAIRS

Although photographing two or three models in one session might seem a daunting prospect for many amateurs, this is an excellent route toward original, challenging compositions, allowing you to explore dynamic relationships and a whole new spectrum of moods. The success of the session will usually be proportionate to the energy you invest in direction. First, get the basic arrangement right, then concentrate on individual poses and expressions. Aim to create a definite bond between the girls – perhaps a shared activity with a prop (for example, folding a sheet) or a common focus of interest (such as the camera itself).

● **Give equal light** to each model, unless you want to place one deliberately in shadow. When using strong natural light from a window, remember that light fall-off may make it impossible to obtain correct exposure for both models, unless they are equidistant from the window.

● **A strong, asymmetric arrangement** is usually the best. Working with two models, try placing them at different distances from the camera. Or try a closely framed double portrait with the heads positioned at different levels.

● **Three models** offer countless opportunities for dynamic groupings. Placing two models close together with the third some distance away can set up an exciting tension. Try focusing selectively to isolate one of the girls.

● **Keep backgrounds simple** to emphasize the relationship between the girls.

● **Use a wide-angle lens** – at least 28mm – to create a sense of depth. This approach works especially well with interiors.

◄ Static poses combined with expressionless stares can help to convey an atmosphere charged with mystery: time itself seems to have stopped in the picture opposite. Although an extreme wide-angle 15mm lens gave me an extensive depth of field, I focused to keep the girl nearest the camera slightly blurred. Diffused flash from the left of the picture supplemented daylight from a window and gave an interesting pallor to the middle girl of the trio.

▲ Makeup can be used to strengthen a facial similarity between two models and set up a visual 'echo', as in the image above. You may find it easier to create such tender, sisterly images if the models already know each other. Remember that an inexperienced, camera-shy girl will often lose her inhibitions if she brings a friend along to pose with her. Identical twins, if you know any, offer marvelous opportunities for mirror effects.

THE ROMANTIC IMAGE

One simple way to make a glamor picture romantic is to choose soft lighting and soft, pastel colors, perhaps adding a soft-focus filter (as described on the following pages). However, all the pictures illustrated on these pages take a more extreme approach: by incorporating suitable costumes, props or settings they make allusions to an idealized world, past or present, or to literature or painting, and in this way suggest a delicate romantic fantasy. Even everyday items such as flowers picked from the garden or a lace shawl can make an important contribution. But always make sure that the model's hairstyle and makeup are consistent with the romantic theme, or the mood will be destroyed.

● **Use fast film** to increase graininess – for example, Ektachrome 200 slide film pushed by two stops. This enriches the atmosphere of a picture. Commercial labs will often push-process film for only a slight extra charge.

● **Avoid overlighting.** Indoors, use daylight controlled by reflectors in preference to flash. Outdoors, choose dawn, dusk or overcast skies, never harsh noonday sun.

● **Background and setting** play a major role. In the studio, choose draped fabrics rather than Colorama paper. Outdoors, a woodland or lakeside setting can be effective. Mist over a lake, or a reflected sunset, intensify the

atmosphere. Historic ruins or grand aristocratic houses also make very romantic backgrounds.

● **Grandmother's clothes** often have a romantic, period flavor; ask your model to bring a selection to the session. Or you can hire historical costumes from a theatrical costumier.

▼ Flowers are the common coinage of romance. You can use them to conjure up pastoral innocence, gypsy warm-bloodedness or the extravagant attentions of a suitor. Just one or two blooms in the hair suffuse a picture with ethereal or passionate connotations. In the left-hand image below I built an elaborate fantasy on the floral theme: an enactment of Ophelia's drowning.

▲ Candlelight suggests old-world glamor, especially if you use it as the sole illumination. But because of its low intensity and high contrast, you will need to take extra care with exposures. For the evocative picture above, I took a reflected light reading from the face and bracketed to be sure of an acceptable result. A typical exposure for a candlelit close-up portrait on ISO 64 film would be $\frac{1}{4}$ second at f/2.

▶ A fast (ISO 500) color slide film used in weak light yielded the attractive sepia tint in this intimate bedroom portrait. To sustain the illusion of a 19th-century photograph, I rigorously excluded all evidence of modernity from the scene. A similar approach is to load black-and-white film and sepia-tone the resulting print. Or with color slide film, it is worth experimenting with brown or sepia filters over the lens.

THE SOFT-FOCUS IMAGE

Soft focus imparts a dreamy quality to a photograph, as if you were looking at the scene through half-closed eyes. To obtain this effect, you cannot simply blur the picture by adjusting the focusing ring. A soft-focus image is essentially sharp, but with slight diffusion of fine detail. This flatters the subject, disguising blemishes and adding a halo to highlights in the eyes, hair and other reflective parts of the image. Colors are also softened and contrast reduced, with an overall gain in atmosphere.

● **Soft-focus attachments** available commercially are inexpensive. They come in different strengths and designs, but most have a central area of sharp focus.

● **Smear a clear filter** lightly with petroleum jelly to improvise your own soft-focus attachment. You can vary the effect by smearing in different patterns. Remember to leave a clear hole in the center.

● **Place fine, gauzy material** in front of the lens as an alternative soft-focus technique. Possibilities include muslin or a nylon stocking. Stretch the material taut over the lens and secure it in place with a rubber band.

● **A word of warning:** don't use a soft-focus attachment every time you want to heighten the mood. This approach, if overdone, can soon degenerate into a photographic cliché.

◄ Breathing on a UV or skylight filter is an easy way to create a soft-focus picture. I took a dozen or so frames of this head-and-shoulders view to obtain different effects as the condensed breath on the filter gradually evaporated in the warm room.

▲ To soften this nude, I used a plastic filter with small bubbles set into it. Another type of soft-focus attachment obtains its effect by an engraved pattern of concentric circles. The spacing of the bubbles or circles governs the degree of diffusion.

THE ART OF THE NUDE

Photographing the female nude is a classic way to celebrate the grace and beauty of the body, in motion or repose. Of course, there is always a sexual content. Some degree of eroticism is legitimate, but the most enduring photographs are those that transcend the blatancy of the girlie magazines and attain some level of artistic seriousness. One rewarding approach is to deploy lighting skills to bring out subtle skin textures or the infinite complexities of 'human geometry'. By closing in on a detail, you can create an image with an impersonal, even abstract quality, despite the intimate nature of the subject matter.

● **Poses and settings** are often a double stumbling block for beginners to nude photography: first attempts may look banal. There are two possible solutions. Either choose simple domestic situations, such as disrobing in a bedroom; or flout naturalism altogether, and create a composition that makes sense in purely pictorial terms.

● **Keep-fit enthusiasts** or keen swimmers, dancers or joggers are excellent subjects for nude studies. They are usually in good physical shape, are used to controlling their bodies, and are more likely to regard their physical attributes objectively. Girls with experience of posing for art classes also tend to be good subjects.

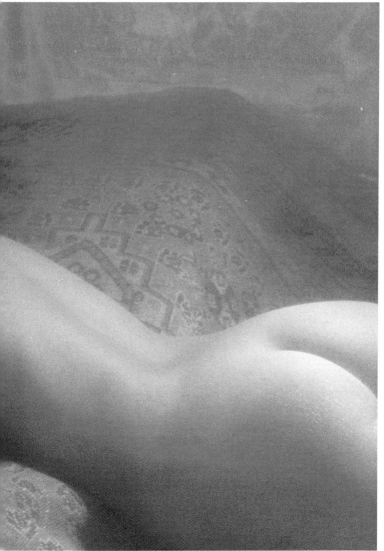

THE FIRST SESSION

Your first photographic session with a nude model need not be daunting if you follow a few simple precepts. One golden rule is to prepare thoroughly. Plan about half a dozen poses, perhaps using the examples in this book to explain what you have in mind: variations will emerge spontaneously as you work together. If you recruit a professional model, you may be tempted to let her take the initiative, and for this reason it is generally more instructive to choose an amateur. Be sensitive to her inhibitions, even if you know her very well, or if she seems full of confidence in other situations.

● **Use daylight,** with reflectors, and load fast film to cope with low lighting. Only try artificial lights when you have had more practice at directing a nude. A warm, private room, with a window that you can cover with diffusing material, is ideal.

● **Loose clothing** worn for several hours before a session will prevent marks on the model's skin caused by underwear elastic or tight waistbands.

● **Start with simple poses,** with one or two props to build up the model's confidence. If she is nervous, reclining poses may help her relax. Taking a few shots while she is still partly clothed can also dispel anxieties.

▲ Natural light makes it easier to concentrate on posing, composition, and camera settings. The pictures above and on the opposite page were taken in afternoon sunlight which streamed through a net curtain over a window. Light bounced off the white walls, so a reflector was unnecessary. The image above shows how a simple prop – the chair – can suggest a pose.

► Rather than switch to an entirely new idea, I continued to explore the standing theme, varying the viewpoint slightly, but taking care not to interrupt the mood. To keep the model as relaxed as possible, I limited the session to natural-looking poses, which she adopted with a minimum of guidance. Constant encouragement and a few compliments did wonders for her confidence.

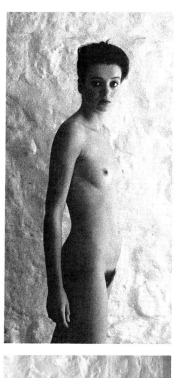

101

BODY TYPES

The photographer of the nude must assess the model objectively, and arrange the elements of the picture to suit her body's individual character. Almost inevitably, there will be weaknesses that you will want to play down. However, avoid too negative an attitude: a picture designed mainly to disguise faults will lack conviction. Choose a pose that shows off the most attractive features, and highlight these by framing and lighting. Do not be limited by fashionable ideas of beauty: if you find generous hips are visually appealing, give them due prominence.

● **Lifting the head back** exaggerates a slender neck.

● **Taking a deep breath** gives a more flattering line to the waist and stomach.

● **A supine pose** flattens large breasts, removing dark shadows and emphasizing line. Stretching the arms up and back does the same.

● **Bending the knees** and elbows stretches the skin and straightens out wrinkles.

● **Long shapely legs** are a tremendous asset. Exaggerate the length of the legs by angling them toward the camera and using a moderately wide-angle lens.

▼ A well-rounded body usually looks better nude than in a clothed, glamor-style picture. The pose below attractively highlights an ample figure.

▼ Soft, directional lighting brings out sinuous body curves in this view of intertwined nudes. To reveal the willowy figures most effectively, I paid particular attention to the position of the models' arms.

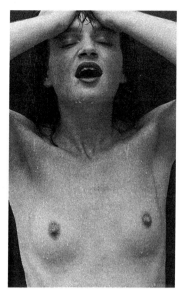

▲ The poses above make an instructive comparison. The frontal pose with arms raised makes the model look flat-chested, emphasizing shape at the expense of form, while the three-quarter view displays a shapely bosom. Actually, both models were similarly proportioned: only the poses make them seem so different. Note how thrusting the hips forward accentuates a slim waist.

▼ Form and shape are given equal emphasis in this pose, which neatly fits a horizontal 35mm format. The pose can be used to make a thin model appear more fleshy, to disguise spare flesh around the stomach, or to hide the neck. In this picture, however, I chose the posture not for purposes of concealment, but to create a sweeping contour along the line of the model's long back.

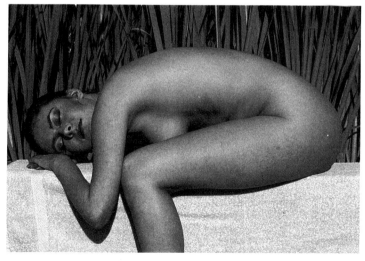

REVEALING FORM

To portray the nude figure as a complex three-dimensional form, the photographer must learn to use light and shadow with great precision, rather as a painter uses a brush. The lighting should be directional, falling across the body so that shadows drift into the hollows, their gradations from dark to light defining the model's contours. You can either use a soft light source for subtle flattery, or a harder oblique light to yield a more contrasty effect that emphasizes the pattern of bones and muscles, perhaps to create a semi-abstract image.

● **A useful exercise** is to set up a single diffused photolamp and observe the balance of light and shadow as you move it around the model. Alter the lamp's height as well as its angle. Then experiment with a reflector added.

● **Toplighting** is usually a good way to show the contours of a reclining nude.

● **Bounce light** onto the model off a white background to create a striking image in which some contours are edged with light while the rest of the body remains in silhouette.

◄ A diffused floodlight, with barndoors attached to narrow the beam, produced just the right lighting quality in the picture opposite – soft enough to moderate the shadows, yet hard enough to show the tensed muscles. Rather than choose a plain background, I felt it would be more interesting to offset the vigorous pose against dim, indistinguishable shapes – actually, items of studio equipment.

▲ For this understated image of gently rounded forms, I used a small tungsten photolamp behind and to the left of the model, aiming it so that the beam raked across her back and buttocks. A reflector angled toward her from the right gave a hint of modeling to the flexed arm and prevented the picture from being more starkly low-key than I wanted. The plain paper background was lit separately.

THE RECLINING NUDE

A recumbent pose has many attractions for the photographer of the nude, the most obvious of which is its evocation of a relaxed, luxurious ambience. Models who feel awkward in standing poses, unable to decide what to do with their hands, often lose their tension when given a comfortable bed, rug or couch to lie on. Moreover, a reclining position offers you great compositional freedom: relieved of their functions as supports, the limbs can be moved into an endless variety of configurations.

● **Couches, benches,** trunks and other structures that you can cover with fabrics or cushions enlarge the choice of reclining poses.

● **A hammock** is a handy accessory for sessions in gardens or woodland locations.

● **A profile view** can be effective if the model bends at least one knee and raises herself on her arms.

● **Spread long hair** over a pillow, carpet or other surface to convey romantic abandon.

● **Use a step ladder** for a high viewpoint; either improvise a camera support with a clamp, or handhold with fast film. Alternatively, use a tripod on a raised, solid surface.

▲ This pose emphasizes taut neck muscles. Petroleum jelly smeared on a UV filter over the lens wrapped the model in a soft haze.

◄ Changes of level multiply the possibilities for dynamic poses – for example, with the back arched. Here, I strengthened the composition further by tilting the camera, which I handheld. Shooting in diffused daylight that streamed into the room through a curtained window, I used Ektachrome 200 film, pushing by two stops; this produced an appropriately grainy effect and softened the colors.

▲ Using a wide-angle lens to exaggerate the foreground works well when you have an attractive floor surface, such as the parquet in this picture. The polished wood reflected a window behind the model and created an aura of light around her. The pose, theatrical lighting effect and simple setting are reminiscent of modern dance. I used a 35mm wide-angle lens, set at a small aperture to extend the depth of field.

BACK VIEWS

A back view of a model invites us to share in her own outlook. If the setting has any depth, we look toward and beyond her, so that in a sense she acquires the function of a framing device, drawing our eye into the picture. In closer views, backs have great appeal because of their subtle contours, to which all too many photographers fail to give due attention. By a careful approach to lighting, you can create strong modeling effects, emphasizing the furrow between the shoulder blades, the ridges of the backbone, or the cleft and curves of the buttocks.

● **Tying up the hair** emphasizes a long, graceful neck.
Alternatively, tie long hair into a pigtail or sweep it over the front of one shoulder.

● **Combine a back view** with a frontal view by posing the model in front of a mirror.

◀ Light from an overcast sky provides delicate modeling in this view of a symmetrical pose within a rural landscape panorama. The jogging pants and the tousled hair give a narrative meaning to the picture, suggesting that the girl is taking a rest after a spell of athletic exercise.

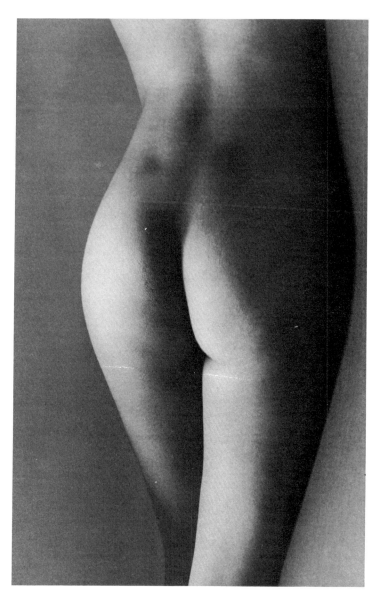

◄ Although this image is carefully posed, the window frame makes it look more like a fortuitous glimpse. The three levels of lighting within the image reinforce the powerful sense of depth, which is additionally strengthened by the outward direction of the girl's gaze.

▲ Soft, directional light from a window was the light source for this close-up. The pleasing lines of the image owe much to the way the left leg continues the generous curves of hip and buttocks, while the gentler curve at the right side of the body provides a subtle counterpoint.

SHOWING DETAILS

Some of the most striking images of the nude are those that show just a part of the body. This approach has both practical and aesthetic advantages. You can disguise a model's less attractive features and concentrate on her good points, and at the same time create powerful, semi-abstract pictures. Simply excluding the face tremendously affects the impact of a nude study, concentrating the eye on forms, shapes and textures while suppressing the competing claims of personality.

● **Close in,** using a long-focus lens to avoid crowding the model. For extreme close-ups, a macro telephoto is useful. At close subject distances or with long-focus lenses, depth of field is reduced. You can maximize depth of field by setting a small aperture, but this demands a longer exposure, with greater risk of a blurred image. So keep your model as still as possible, providing an out-of-frame support, such as a chair or table, for her to lean on.

● **Use nail paint** to introduce color accents that stand out against flesh tones.

▼ Cropping the head always focuses more attention on skin texture and body forms.

► Fingertips touching the body strongly evoke the tactile sensations. Make sure that the nails are well manicured. By keeping some of the fingers out of focus, as in the picture immediately at right, you can help to convey movement.

▼ The scale is not always immediately apparent in close-ups of the body. Unusual poses such as this help you to exploit the viewer's confusion.

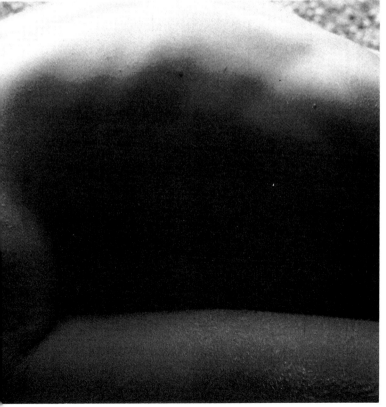

REVEALING SHAPE

The classic nude study dwells on rounded, sculptural forms, but you can also celebrate the body by taking the opposite tack – that of suppressing form and instead taking shape (that is, pure outline) as your main subject. The key to this strategy is to eliminate or soften the subtle gradations of shadow that define volume. You can either exploit backlighting to reduce the body to a silhouette, or arrange a studio lighting scheme to create a shadowless or near-shadowless image. Either way, keep the poses simple: a pose that works well in three dimensions will often look merely confusing when flattened to two dimensions.

● **Create a silhouette** by placing the model between the camera and a bright light source, such as a window looking onto brilliant sunlight. Expose for the background. Load slow slide film, which has a narrower exposure latitude than faster film. Silhouettes offer an excellent entrée into nude photography, allowing you to concentrate on shape to the exclusion of more complicated elements.

● **Combine a silhouette** with a translucent detail such as a hair comb or glass of red wine, positioned so as to allow light to pass through. This can lead to strikingly original images.

● **Reduce modeling** with broad diffused lighting from near the camera position – for example, a pair of floodlights with sheets of tracing paper stretched in front.

▶ When shape is paramount, choose graphic poses, using elbows, knees or other joints to make sharp angles that offset the curves. For the upper two pictures opposite, I asked the model to hold a pose. But for the lower image I exposed a sequence of frames in rapid succession while the girl walked along a wall. I relied on chance to provide a pleasingly shaped silhouette of the nude; but to be sure of obtaining the correct exposure, I staged two repeat performances, bracketing above and below a meter reading from the sky.

▼ This nude detail is an arresting study in symmetry. But to avoid too static an image, I framed so that the torso is slightly off-center, with one elbow cropped. Soft front lighting lightened the shadows, emphasizing shapes but without reducing the modeling too much.

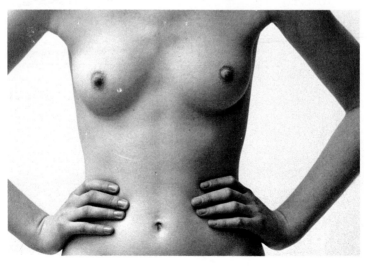

113

EMPHASIZING SKIN

Successful nude studies often owe their appeal to their tactile quality: they convey the feel of skin to the touch. To achieve such sensuous images, accurate camera technique is essential, as the slightest degree of camera shake, misfocusing or wrong exposure will militate against the *crispness* of the image and obscure textural details. The pictures on these two pages depend as much on meticulous technique as on the use of water or suntan oil to add interest to the skin's texture.

● **Use slow film** to reduce grain to a minimum. A tripod always improves image quality, even when there is enough available light for a handheld shot.

● **Use soft, directional light** (for example, from a window or diffused photolamp) to do justice to subtle textures.

▶ A coating of suntan oil gives the skin an attractive sheen. Here, I used a reflector to direct raking sunlight onto the torso. Back-lighting picked out the fine down.

▼ I framed close on this contrast of textures. Oiling the skin and sprinkling it with water droplets is always effective.

THE SEMI-NUDE

It is perhaps ironic that many models who are shy of appearing completely nude are happy to pose in lingerie or skimpy garments that heighten rather than subdue the eroticism. How overtly sexual you make your semi-nude pictures is a matter over which only you – and the model, of course – can legislate. However, beginners often confuse the erotic with the vulgar – and in the process miss opportunities for images that are charged with sensuality, yet still perfectly valid in artistic terms. Props, such as the sunglasses below, can sometimes be used to add an erotic charge.

● **A detailed setting,** such as a bedroom, provides a realistic context for a partially dressed model. Aim at a candid approach, with the model absorbed in her own thoughts or activities. Underexpose to enrich the atmosphere, throw bedroom clutter into shadow and emphasize folds of bed linen, sleepwear or lingerie.

● **A plain or abstract background** is suited to either provocative poses inspired by striptease, or to bold compositions with strong textural or color contrasts between skin and fabrics.

● **White or cream lingerie,** if it occupies a large proportion of the picture frame, may mislead the exposure meter and cause skin tones to appear dark. Take a close-up reflected light reading from the skin, or an incident light reading.

▲ Foliage motifs on the gauzy curtain through which I took this photograph echo and amplify the lace texture of the panties. Below, the rich blue tones of denim add impact to a graphic close-up.

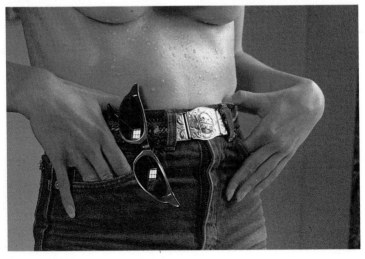

▲ This silky gown and glimpse of drapes suggest a bedroom context: we feel that we are meeting the girl on her own territory. By contrast, the coy tug at the vest (below) involves us in flirtation. Right, I used a semi-clothed model in a more passive role. Remember, you can use clothes to highlight parts of the body, as well as hide them (below, right).

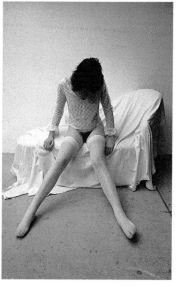

THE MONOCHROME NUDE 1

In black-and-white photographs, the nude tends to become more impersonal, even to the point of abstraction. One of the most satisfying approaches is to intensify this effect, choosing compositions and lighting schemes that create assertive shapes and patterns, without necessarily making any concessions to realism. Whatever the desired mood, you should have a strong, positive idea about the picture. Black-and-white images that are technically good but lacking in imaginative conviction will invariably appear dull and disappointing.

● **Use lighting** (and dodging or burning in during enlargement) to offset pale flesh tones against a black background, or dark or suntanned skin against white.

● **Try eliminating midtones** to create a dramatic study in pure volume. Load fast film and choose a hard, contrasty lighting scheme.

● **To flatter skin tones,** avoid too much contrast or sharpness. One way is to place fine nylon mesh over the enlarger lens during printing.

● **Experiment freely** with unconventional viewpoints, poses, lighting effects, backgrounds, props and camera settings.

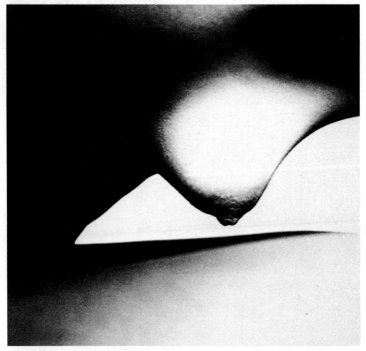

▲ For this close-up I used harsh lighting, and selective shading during enlargement. You can take this 'minimal' approach further, exploiting the visual confusions to which black-and-white lends itself – perhaps even making the body resemble a landscape.

▶ The low-key lighting in this image was created by a single spotlight which I placed to the left of the camera. To prevent light from being reflected onto the model's back from a white wall behind her, I strategically fixed up a sheet of black cardboard.

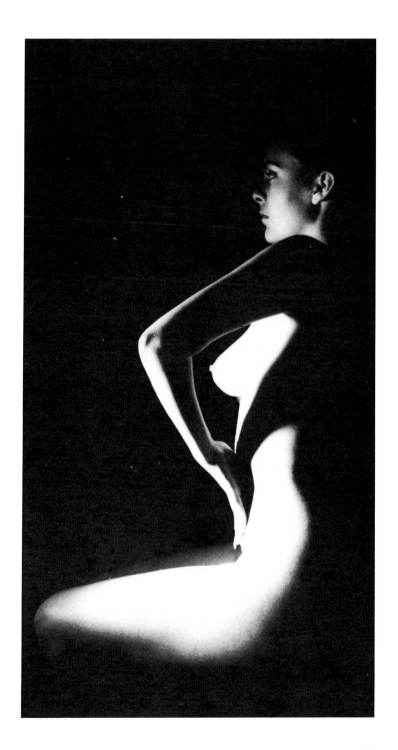

THE MONOCHROME NUDE 2

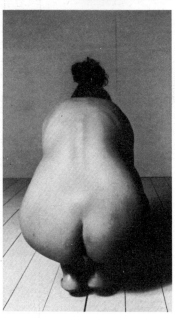

▲ Clothing the torso with shadow patterns is a classic way to reveal the subtleties of form. If I had included the eyes in this example, they would have deflected attention away from the delicate tracery.

◄ Bare walls and floorboards can form an impressively austere setting for the black-and-white nude. Here, I used a specially built set, whose converging lines counterpoint with the huddled, pear-shaped body.

► Although morning daylight diffused through a net curtain produced natural-looking modeling, the strength of this picture lies equally in its unnatural aspects – for example, the breadth of the hips, exaggerated by a wide-angle lens. The coathangers, hooks and the vertical lines of the door create a frame that leads the eye restlessly around the image.

121

SETTING AND VIEWPOINT

It is sometimes helpful to remind yourself that the camera's view is highly selective, even through a wide-angle lens. By judicious choice of viewpoint, you can create stunning pictures from a setting that at first seems unpromising, or use details to hint at a broader context. With close framing, just a small patch of garden could be used to evoke a woodland, or even a tropical location. Indoors, the range of viewpoints is more restricted – but with the compensation that you can re-arrange furnishings, or add or subtract elements, to create a background that perfectly complements the model in a wholly unified composition.

● **In rural settings,** there is often a temptation to rely on the beauty or grandeur of the landscape to guarantee stunning pictures. Guard against this danger. Pay as much attention to details of dress, hair, pose and expression as you would in a studio setting. Check carefully in the viewfinder for obtrusive details such as garbage or overhead wires.

● **In the home,** familiarity can blunt your powers of observation when you look around for suitable settings. Try to appraise each room or detail with a fresh eye. Don't restrict yourself to the lounge or bedroom. For example, you could try using the staircase, where you can exploit the change of level to extend your range of camera angles.

SIMPLE BACKGROUNDS

In theory, the studio photographer's control over background is absolute; in practice, cost and time impose limitations. The best plan is to collect a dozen or so rolls of plain or simply patterned papers and fabrics that are wide enough for full-length portraiture, as well as keeping photographic needs in mind whenever you redecorate your home. White walls or background papers are surprisingly versatile: by lighting the background separately and placing colored gel over the lamps, you can easily change the hue.

● **Colorama papers,** specially made for photographers, are sold in rolls 9 feet (2¾ meters) wide. Thread a pole through the core of the roll and mount this on a pair of stands; a homemade stand is shown on page 23. Mounting several rolls on one stand allows you to switch backgrounds easily. Tear off any scuffed or wrinkled paper before each session.

● **Wallpaper offcuts** are often sold cheaply. You can quicky paper a large sheet of plywood, choosing a pattern that complements or counterpoints the model's clothes.

● **Alter the tones** of a plain background by adjusting the lighting. For variety, try throwing graphic shadows.

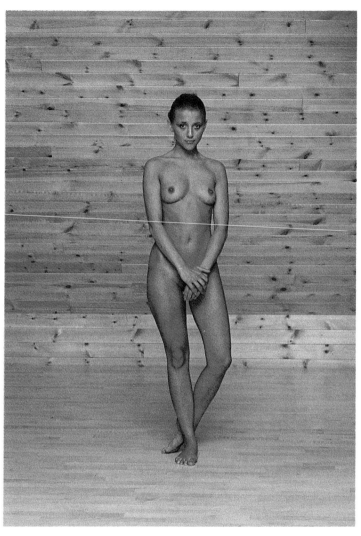

◄ Pulling down Colorama paper in a gentle sweep to the floor creates a horizonless background, as in the top picture opposite. To prevent the model from casting shadows, I lit the background separately, angling two diffused lamps so that their beams crossed just behind her. By contrast the lower picture has a flat canvas background which I spray-painted in free-form shapes to suggest stylized clouds. The sunglasses create a summery mood.

▲ Distinctive textures such as those of wood, brickwork or stonework can make superb backgrounds, but to exploit them you must normally be prepared to venture outside the studio. In this full-length nude, photographed in a gymnasium, the horizontal lines of the pine panelling accentuate the body's curves, while the wood's rich brown tone complements suntanned skin. The monochrome background draws attention to the blue eye makeup.

ELABORATE BACKGROUNDS

When planning a background or set for a studio session, you can save time, expense and space by paying close attention to scale and viewpoint: there is no need to extend a set much beyond the edges of the viewfinder frame. Remember, too, that well-chosen props can often be more evocative than a background painted with meticulous realism. Even quite lavish-looking room sets can be built from just a couple of screens, a floor covering, perhaps a small area of ceiling, and one or two items of furniture or simple extras such as plants or mirrors.

● **Make a scale drawing** to plan the dimensions of a set. Put in the walls of the studio or room, and the angle of view of the widest lens you intend to use. Professional photographers often draw the main lines of their plan in chalk on the floor before assembling screens and props. Alternatively, you can use string stretched taut, or low-tack masking tape.

● **To make wall flats,** use hardboard sheets fixed to timber frames. Join these panels together either by screws or clamps. Polystyrene is also good for set-building: it is inexpensive, lightweight, and can be bought as sheets, blocks or tiles.

● **Rolls of felt,** available in a range of colors, can be used to simulate fine-quality carpets.

▲ The background to this room set (shown uncropped to reveal the construction) was a wallpapered sheet of hardboard at right angles to the studio wall. Timber struts gave rear support. If you wish, you can introduce fittings such as a light switch to add to the authenticity.

▶ Sometimes, a stagy background can be more atmospheric than attempted naturalism. For this simulated barn interior, I used a painted canvas with real hay bales. To match the illusion of sun streaming through the window, I chose soft, diffused lighting that imitated daylight.

▲ By using slides to make projected backgrounds, you can simulate outdoor locations in a home studio. For the picture above I hired a specialist front-projection unit, but you can obtain similar effects by back projection, with an ordinary projector positioned behind the screen and the model in front. The screen should be thin enough to show the image clearly but thick enough to prevent a hot spot in the middle. Special acrylic screens are available, but an alternative is a large sheet of thick tracing paper stretched over a wood frame. Use barndoors or snoots to prevent the lighting on the model from spilling onto the projected image. Balance the studio lighting to the quality and direction of the lighting in the slide for a natural effect.

INTERIORS

In an indoor setting, you should allow yourself plenty of time to move furniture and clear away clutter, especially for wide-angle views. Sometimes, you may prefer the atmospheric and pictorial impact of a room full of bric-à-brac. However, avoid overwhelming the model with a mass of details. To isolate her within the composition, ensure that the light she receives is stronger than the light falling elsewhere within the room.

● **Lighten dark corners** with diffused or bounced flash. Keep flash units out of sight behind furniture or in alcoves. Trigger with slave units, to avoid cables appearing in the picture.

● **Exaggerated perspective** caused by a downward-tilted camera with a wide-angle lens usually looks more acceptable than when the camera has been tilted toward the ceiling. But to keep vertical lines parallel, ensure that the camera is level.

● **A wall mirror** may reflect unwanted details. If so, try changing its angle by wedging a film box between its lower edge and the wall. Or spray the surface with a film of water.

▼ When space is restricted, try shooting from a neighboring room, using a doorway as a framing device.

▲ A detail of a room can be just as successful as a broader view. In this picture – an apparent dislocation of the female form – the wall mirror serves to convey depth.

▲ Grand architecture provides an opulent setting for glamor (above and below). Owners can sometimes be persuaded to allow you access for photo sessions.

▼ Photographing interiors by available light gives the most natural-looking results. Here, though, I used a photolamp, overlighting for a cold effect.

GLAMOR ON LOCATION

Although location photography often places you at the mercy of changing light and weather, its overriding attraction is infinite variety. Even driving on weekly sessions to sites within an hour from home, you will never exhaust all the possibilities. And if your wife or girlfriend models for you, weekend breaks or longer vacations provide an exciting chance to use less familiar settings in images that combine two photographic genres – glamor and travel – for spectacular results.

● **Plan a timetable** in detail. Take the light into account: it is disastrous to arrive at a site just as the sun sinks behind a hill or a tall building.

● **Provide changing facilities** and a mirror. In the countryside, you can improvise a dressing room with tent poles and canvas.

● **For vacation glamor,** keep your outfit light, but don't leave the tripod behind.

● **Use details occasionally,** even when broader views offer more obvious possibilities.

▼ Grand architecture conveys opulence; this picture shows a building in Barcelona. More mundane sites, such as the slate quarry (below, left), can have a gritty realism that highlights the glamor by providing a contrast.

▼ Try matching clothes to background. Below, the flowers embroidered on the tunic seem to have been plucked from the garden itself; while in the image below, right, the anorak echoes the poolside wall behind.

▲ It is important to choose a viewpoint that makes best use of a location's qualities. Here, I revealed a swirling pattern in the storm-flattened corn by standing on a wall and pointing the camera downward.

WATER

Lakeside or seaside locations offer a sense of spaciousness, combined with attractive lighting effects when early or late sun scatters reflected highlights. Or in the more enclosed setting of a pool, you can ask a nude or swimsuited model to float relaxedly (perhaps with a suitable prop), swim underwater for graceful distortions of the body's shape, or splash around vigorously for dramatic action shots.

● **Keep equipment dry.** A UV or skylight filter protects lenses from splashes. Sea spray is corrosive; to avoid damage, put the camera in a plastic bag with the lens uncovered, and seal with a rubber band.

● **Turbulence** exaggerates the fragmented appearance of bodies underwater. Try agitating the surface of the water to exploit this effect creatively.

● **Use a polarizing filter** to cut down glare and saturate the blue of the water.

● **Underwater housings** are specially made for SLR cameras. Use one with a snorkel and face mask to obtain dramatic shots from below the surface.

▲ Dividing a picture into equal sky and sea often creates too static a composition. But here the symmetry is offset by the model's position in the frame. To bring the foam into view, I used a 24mm lens. Adding a half-stop to the meter reading made the highlights more brilliant while keeping the girl in semi-silhouette.

◄ In a predominantly blue seascape, a red color accent always looks effective. Here, I restricted the color scheme by excluding the foreground – the jetty where the girl was standing. As in the picture above this one, I used the model as a link between sea and sky. The yacht adds a further vertical element that helps unify the image. Setting a wide aperture, I blurred the boat slightly to avoid deflecting interest from the girl.

▲ Before arranging a pool session, make sure that your model has all the skills required for the shots you have in mind. For pictures like the one above, it is not enough for her to say merely that she can swim: she must be absolutely at home in the water. A diving board makes an excellent viewpoint for such images, allowing you to concentrate on the varied shapes made by the swimmer and to exclude any distracting poolside features.

THE NUDE OUTDOORS

A nude in a landscape is an inspiring theme, perhaps because we all feel the tug of back-to-nature romanticism. Wild settings, such as seaside cliffs, deserts, forests or mountains, can impart an exhilarating sense of freedom to a nude photograph, and also have the advantage of privacy. In country areas, make sure that you keep away from paths used by hikers and riders. City-dwellers may prefer locations nearer home: a garden, rooftop, balcony or private pool could be ideal. If there is a risk of being observed, you may be able to prevent this by careful use of screens.

● **Anticipate the weather.** Remember, it will often be much cooler in the mountains or by the sea. Take a thick robe to keep the model warm before and after a photo session.

● **Carry insect repellant** and antiseptic cream. Stay clear of areas where insects can be especially troublesome.

● **Avoid onlookers** by working just after dawn in summer. The soft, oblique light will reveal form.

● **Check the law** when photographing on holidays abroad. In some countries, even modest bodily exposure is illegal.

● **Use rocky settings** or pebble beaches to contrast with soft skin.

◄ A craggy wilderness and a well-trimmed lawn offer contrasting settings for the same model. Garden furniture is often a good source of props. For the upper picture I used a 28mm lens to increase the sense of spaciousness and dramatize the pose.

▲ Woods provide useful seclusion. In early-morning or late-afternoon sunlight, the interplay of light and shadow supplies atmosphere and compositional interest. And you only have to move a few yards to gain a fresh range of background options.

THE ORIGINAL APPROACH

Photography is a marvelous vehicle for the imagination. To exploit
the full potential for creating fantasies and novel effects, there are
various devices you can use. These range from the camera controls
themselves, to all kinds of photographic items (such as projectors or
special-effects filters), to simple household objects such as mirrors.
Experiment freely, and take plenty of creative risks. Often, the
results will be entirely unpredictable. For this reason, you should
never be too stinting with film. The compensation for a higher failure
rate than you are used to will be at least a sprinkling of images that
startle or baffle the eye.

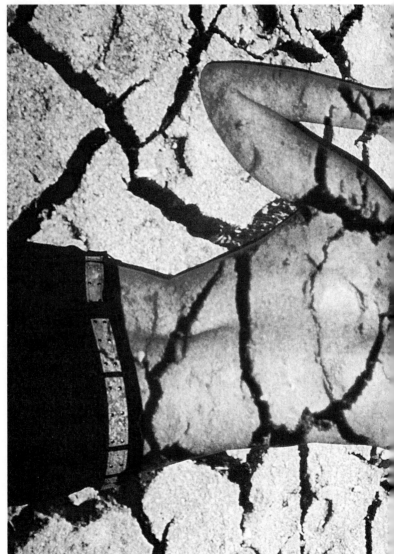

● **Defy the conventions** of photography if you feel that this will strengthen a picture's impact. Sometimes, you can add a sense of movement by turning the camera at an angle – even if this produces a tilted horizon. Try out 'incorrect' camera settings and unorthodox lighting, aiming for mystery or drama instead of a naturalistic effect.

● **Improvise special effects** from materials you have to hand. For example, you could use a translucent candy wrapper as a colored filter. Or by cutting a half-circle out of black cardboard and fitting it as a revolvable mask over the lens, you can make a selective double exposure so that the same model appears twice in a single picture.

COMBINATIONS

Combining two slides to make a composite image (or 'sandwich') can be a profitable avenue of experiment. Unlike combinations made from black-and-white negatives, sandwiches require no darkroom facilities – just an eye for a good match. Another approach, which leads to pictures that are sometimes indistinguishable from sandwiches when projected, is to expose two images on the same frame of film. Yet a third possibility is to project a slide onto a background, introduce some new element into the scene, and then photograph the result.

● **To make a sandwich,** choose two slides that are slightly over-exposed, or the composite image may look too dark. Judge the effect of the combination by superimposing the slides on a light box. Then, using a craft knife, remove the slides from their mounts, tape them together along one edge, and remount the sandwich. You can show the resulting image in a viewer, project it, or duplicate it in a slide copier. Alternatively, you can send the sandwich to a photo lab for printing.

● **To make a double exposure** is easy if your camera has a double exposure lever allowing you to override the device that prevents you from taking two shots on one frame inadvertently. If you lack this facility, follow the procedure diagrammed opposite.

▼ Avoid sandwiching slides that are full of detail, or the image may look cluttered. Attempts at a naturalistic result usually fail: it is better to create surreal fantasies. Below, I combined a portrait with a blurred view of trees.

▲ Double exposures work best when there is only a limited area of overlap between the images, as above. Dark areas in one subject allow details of the other subject to show through clearly. The classic use of this effect is to add a romantic moon to a portrait with a dark background.

▼ Discrepancies of scale can sometimes add to the impact of a composite image. I created this one by projecting onto a white wall a slide showing a girl in a sweater outlined against the sky. With a semi-nude model posed in front of the projected image, I then photographed the arrangement.

▲ To combine two images on one frame, the first step is to take up any slack in the film by turning the rewind knob. Then press in the rewind release to free the sprocket wheels that normally advance the film between exposures. Lastly, advance the wind-on lever without letting go of either the rewind knob or the rewind release. This procedure will cock the shutter for a second exposure without winding on.

FANTASY LIGHTING

In the studio, dramatic lighting can be a substitute for a background or set, or a way to create original images in which the model is subordinate to a visual concept based on pattern or color. The latter approach is useful if your model's attributes do not conform to conventional ideas of glamor, or when you want to unleash your imagination.

● **Colored gels** over the light source enable you to control the color content effectively. White areas will become indistinguishable from areas that have the same hue as the colored light source, while colors complementary to the lighting will darken to black. Two gels of complementary hue (such as magenta and green) will create white light where the beams overlap, revealing these areas in their true colors.

● **Bounce a floodlight** or spotlight off a colored wall or sheet of colored paper as an alternative way to add color.

● **Create a green glow** and make skin tones seem unearthly by loading daylight film and shooting in fluorescent light.

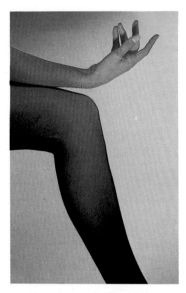

▼ Projecting a slide onto a model creates complex, distorted images. Below, I used a slide of an op-art painting, which echoed the painted op-art background.

▲ A floodlight covered with green gel illuminated a sheet of thin paper from behind to form the background to this image. Red gel over the main light tinted the legs.

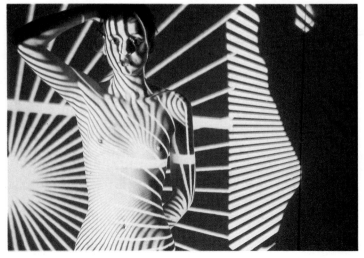

► Colored spotlights can be used to add elliptical areas of color to a background. By altering the lighting angle you can elongate an ellipse or squash it to a circle. In this picture, the background was a projection screen.

▼ This is a more elaborate color fantasy. The background was a large sheet of black velvet. I opened the shutter on the camera's B setting and fired a flash unit to record the model and the man's head leaning out from behind her. Then, during a two-minute time exposure the man whirled colored torches around, which recorded as light trails. Before closing the shutter, I fired the flash again. This time the man was hidden behind the model; she had moved slightly, and thus appears as a double image in the resulting transparency.

SPECIAL-EFFECTS FILTERS

Dozens of different special-effects filters are now available, at easily affordable prices. It is well worth experimenting with these attachments, even if only occasionally, to invest your nude and glamor pictures with an unreal, dreamlike quality. You can employ filters to transform either color or composition. The results may be relatively muted – for example, when you add a fog filter to soften the details and hues in a picture, or a graduated filter to give a stormy, threatening look to a sky. However, you can also achieve much more radical effects, fragmenting the image, scattering it with starbursts or rainbows, or framing the model with an iris of bright color or kaleidoscopic patterns.

● **Starburst filters** spread light from bright highlights to create sparkling rays, as at left.

● **Diffraction filters** break up highlights into streaks, stars or wheels of blue, green and red.

● **Prism filters** multiply parts of the image in radial patterns, or in parallel bands that can suggest vigorous movement.

● **Center-spot filters** create a soft-focus vignette around a central clear portion. Color-spot filters use the same principle to create a colored vignette.

● **Strong color filters** can deceive your camera's TTL meter. Take a reading without the filter in position, and increase the exposure by the manufacturer's recommended 'filter factor'.

◄ Starburst filters add romantic twinkles to reflected highlights on glass, metal or water, or to city lights or candles. The top image, opposite, has a six-pointed star on the illuminated ring, but you can also buy filters that produce two, four or eight stars. Graduated filters are mostly used to add color to skies, as in the picture, left. Because the transition from clear to colored is gradual, the effect is relatively subtle.

▲ You can use various kinds of prism filter to frame the model with ghosted forms (top, left) or break up the whole image into a scrambled pattern (above). Use your depth of field preview control: with prism filters, as with many other kinds, the effect will depend on the aperture you set. The pool picture here shows a simpler composition: by fitting a center-spot filter, I gave the impression of a theatrical spotlight.

TRICKS WITH FILM

One fruitful route toward a more avant-garde, experimental kind of glamor photography is to choose special films, or special processing methods, in order to show the female form in a strange new light. Particularly vivid effects are possible with mismatched processing – that is, applying to one type of film the processing chemistry designed for a different type. You can also use purely physical techniques, such as heat treatment, to manipulate the appearance of a slide or print in a controlled, artistic fashion.

● **Infrared color film,** which is sensitive to both radiation and visible light, produces vibrant color effects. It is designed for use with a No. 12 yellow filter, which makes skin appear waxy and greenish and vegetation appear red. Set a narrow aperture, or the image may appear out of focus. Bracket generously.

▼ You can transform a Polaroid SX-70 instant color print by rubbing a blunt-ended instrument over its surface during the processing stage. This moves the dyes around in the emulsion. Below, I used this method to turn a mundane background into a pattern of squiggles that focuses attention on the nude.

● **Infrared black-and-white film** makes skin appear unreal and darkens the eyes. Water and sky record as black. Store the film in a freezer until needed. Load and unload in total darkness. Use with a deep red (No. 70) or visually opaque (No. 87) filter. Use your lens's special IR focusing index.

● **Try printing a slide** onto color negative paper instead of reversal paper – or ask a lab to do so. The result will be a negative print, with high contrast and brilliant reversed colors. (The color reversal is not exact, as slides, unlike color negatives, do not have an orange color-correcting mask.)

● **Try processing slide film** in color, negative chemicals to yield negative transparencies. For good results, avoid over-contrasty lighting, and bracket exposures.

▼ I made this negative print in my own darkroom from a color transparency. Instead of enlarging from the slide onto color reversal paper in the usual way, I enlarged onto black-and-white printing paper. If you do not have access to an enlarger, you can order negative prints from a lab. Nudes are particularly suited to this treatment, because the reversal of tones emphasizes form and suppresses competing claims of personality.

TRICKS WITH MOVEMENT

Moving the camera during a long exposure, or asking the model to move, can create an impressionistic effect. Details are softened and confused, colors merge, and highlights spread bright trails across the image. The results of such creative strategies are never totally predictable, so you should be prepared to shoot several rolls of film, varying the camera settings and the speed of movement to be sure of getting at least a handful of striking images. For example, you could try setting a slow shutter speed and panning the camera to follow the model as she moves across your field of view.

● **In daylight,** a meter may indicate a fast shutter speed even at the smallest aperture setting. To allow a slower speed, fit a neutral density filter over the lens to cut down the amount of light entering the camera.

● **Zooming** during a long exposure (that is, turning the focal length ring) creates a radiating blur around the subject.

● **For a controlled blur,** set the camera on a tripod and tilt or rotate the head during exposure.

▼ The composition below is enlivened by vivid streaks of color. I achieved this effect by asking all but one of the models to run across the field of view, from the right. A shutter speed of one second blurred them to ghostly forms.

▲ A limited area of movement can often be effective. Here, I used a glowing sweep of highlights to convey the sparkle of a night-club. The effect was caused by a wineglass, which a companion moved swiftly back toward him after drinking a toast.

▲ Tilting the camera in a short vertical arc during a half-second exposure produced this unusual image. The blurred background resembles brushstrokes, making the photograph look rather like a painting.

▼ The model twisted her head very slightly to add a hint of a blur to the evocative portrait below, taken at a shutter speed of 1/8 on Ektachrome 400 slide film, which I pushed two stops to improve atmosphere.

MONTAGE

Montage is the technique of combining portions of different prints to create one composite image – usually, a fantasy picture that you could not obtain simply by photographic means. The normal procedure is to mount a large print on stiff cardboard to form a base, onto which you then paste smaller cut-outs. If scale is crucial, you will probably need to have prints specially made to the right size; take a carefully sized sketch of the intended montage to your photo lab, along with the negatives. Before pasting down the cut-out images, darken their edges with soft pencil. After assembly, photograph the end-result to yield a master negative; prints made from this should show no sign of joins.

● **Choose prints** that are made on the same grade of paper and are matched in density and contrast.

● **To disguise joins,** first cut out each print with scissors, leaving an inch to spare all around. Score round your chosen outline with a craft knife, just piercing the emulsion. Now make a series of flaps by cutting right through the print from this outline to the cut edges. By pulling on each flap, remove backing paper to yield a cut-out with thin edges. Smooth irregularities with fine sandpaper.

● **Paste cut-outs** in place with a non-stain spray adhesive.

● **Retouch** cut edges if necessary. On black-and-white montages, use a felt pen, or gouache diluted to the appropriate tone. On color montages, use colored gouache.

▼ To create the double-image montage below, I departed from the usual method and used slides instead of prints. After cutting the two slides in half, I butted opposite halves together, and printed the resulting hybrid.

▲ Combining different views of
one model can be a rewarding
approach. Above, I used eight
prints, delicately retouched.

▼ Dramatic juxtaposition of scale
can be an exciting aspect of
montage. This example also
exploits a contrast of textures.

HIDING THE FACE

There is no limit to the ways you can conceal the face in a glamor shot to create a more intriguing image. Perhaps the most successful pictures in this mould are those where we feel that the features have only just been hidden – a moment or two earlier and we would not have been so tantalized. For the photographer, such concealment has a practical aspect: it frees him from worrying about the model's expression.

● **Use props,** details of the setting, or the model's hair, hands, arms or clothing to conceal the face. Alternatively, set a slow shutter speed and ask the model to move her head slightly so that it records on film as a blur, but with a distinct outline.

● **Include the eyes,** but disguise the rest of the face, for a powerful effect that directly involves the viewer. You could do this by photographing the face through a venetian blind, or alternatively by showing just the eyes in a strip of mirror or other highly reflective surface.

▼ Sunglasses with mirror-like lenses are good for special effects. Below, I held white cardboard in front of the model, so that the lenses would reflect pure white. Overexposure disguised skin texture to heighten the mystery.

▲ The ornate handmirror harmonizes with this model's costume, while its circular shape is repeated in the wristwatch. To make a graphic picture, I held up the sari on a thread of cotton invisible to the camera.

▼ A portrait in which the mouth betrays emotion while the eyes are hidden has a profound impact. Below, I concentrated this impact by framing close with a 90mm lens, simplifying the background and using makeup expressively.

▲ This girl's face is obscured by wind-blown hair, yet her eyes, nose and mouth are just discernible. Indoors, a fan or wind machine can give the same effect. Below, I used foliage for concealment instead of hair.

SCREENS

A screen in front of the lens can simplify a face or figure into a graphic shape, or superimpose an attractive or mysterious texture upon a recognizable image. Virtually any meshed, clear or translucent material will serve. Screens are abundant in the home; you could experiment with frosted glass in the bathroom, or a lacy curtain or tablecloth. Or with a little extra effort, you can make your own screens – perhaps by dotting a sheet of glass with colored paints or with the stick-on spots of colored paper sold by stationery or department stores.

● **The effect of a screen** depends on the focal length of the lens, its aperture, and the distance from lens to screen. For example, moving the screen toward the lens makes the picture more diffuse.

● **An open-textured screen,** such as a piece of lace or a venetian blind, can be used to throw shadows onto the model that echo the pattern of the screen itself.

● **Rain-spattered windows** can make effective screens. To simulate raindrops, flick water onto a window vigorously with a brush.

● **Boil a kettle** near a window to exploit the diffusing effect of steamed-up glass. Drops of condensed steam trickling down the window will break up the image into vertical bands.

▼ Mesh fabric screens impart a cocooned, intimate feel. It is easy to rig up a screen using household material: stretch string across the room and attach the fabric with clothes pegs. Below, I used a mosquito net that completely surrounded the reclining nude, giving the picture an ambiguous air of protection and captivity that strengthens its impact.

▶ A curved sheet of translucent plastic filtered out detail from this girl's features and dress and gracefully elongated her neck. The sheet also served as a reflector, throwing some light from the window back onto the figure to reveal a few clues to appearance – the eyes, the lips and the scattering of flowers in the dress.

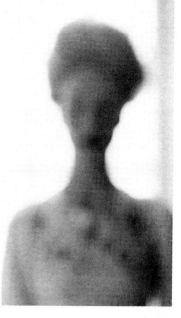

▼ In both pictures below, I combined screens with reflections in glass to create a deliberate spatial confusion. The indistinct backgrounds – my studio, and a conservatory full of greenery – increase the mystery. In the left-hand image, ceiling lamps highlight the condensation on the window, which evokes a wintry day. The impact of the right-hand image depends largely on the angled viewpoint; if I had photographed square-on to the venetian blinds, the picture would have looked much more static.

REFLECTIONS

We are all entranced by reflections, not just out of vanity, but also because of some deep-rooted magic that mirror images exert. In nude and glamor photography, mirrors are particularly appropriate as props or backgrounds, in the context of dressing, combing or adjusting hair, or applying makeup. They allow you to show the face or figure from altered viewpoints, or to cast the viewer adrift in spatial mysteries. Remember also that there are many other types of reflective material, with which you can experiment freely to yield exciting special effects – for example, windows, reflective foil (which you can crumple or curve for bizarre distortions), even car bumpers or hubcaps.

● **Focusing** on a reflection requires care. For focusing purposes, a reflected image is the same distance behind the mirror as the subject is in front of the mirror. To keep all three planes in focus – the model, the mirror frame, and the model's reflection – set a narrow aperture. An alternative approach is to blur the model deliberately by setting a wide aperture and focusing on the reflection. Either way, use the camera's depth of field preview control if it has one.

● **A reflection of yourself** and the camera may appear in the image inadvertently. Check the viewfinder carefully. If you cannot move the camera without spoiling the composition, make it as unobtrusive as possible and photograph from outside the field of view using a cable release.

● **Sunglasses** can add a novel touch to a portrait if they reflect the surrounding scene. The secret is to keep the model in the shade and set the minimum aperture.

● **When using flash,** beware of hard, bright reflections off mirrors. These will appear as burned-out highlights.

● **Mirrors** indoors offer a way to extend the subject distance when space is restricted.

▼ Reflective silver or gold foil is well worth adding to your collection of studio background papers. Two different uses are shown in the images below.

▲ This bathtime frolic, which I photographed with a 24mm lens set at f/16, is a tongue-in-cheek fantasy. Two walls of mirrors multiply the figures from four to twelve – thirteen if you include my own partial reflection, which I included in the composition for deliberate effect. The mirrors also serve as efficient reflectors, increasing the available light in the scene. Dressing-table mirrors with side flaps offer similar, though less spectacular chances for multiple effects.

▼ This dignified portrait shows the value of selective focusing. I used slow black-and-white film to record the girl's attractively freckled face very sharply, but set the 90mm lens at a wide aperture – f/4 – to blur the reflection slightly; this eliminated the freckles. Coming in close to exclude the mirror frame strengthened the impact of this illusion. A sheet of black velvet reflected in the mirror supplies a featureless background that accentuates the faces.

VISUAL ECHOES

Bizarre juxtapositions can be a rich source of wit – a quality I would recommend to the many glamor photographers who take themselves and their subjects too seriously. The pictures here generate gentle humor from an unlikely visual echo between the model and her surroundings. Creating images like these requires not only keen observation, but also an ability to make strong, simple compositions, uncluttered by irrelevant details that would obscure the central message.

● **Statues** offer potential for comic imitation. Use poses, clothes or props to echo a particular aspect of the statue. Such juxtapositions are reinforced by the contrast of a youthful body against antique stone.

● **Patterned fabrics** sometimes have motifs that you can echo in the background to a picture. For example, a dress with a pattern of palm trees might be amusing in a desert context. Examine the model's wardrobe: a particular garment may well spark off a picture idea.

▶ Geometry provides the basis for humor in this picture – one of a long sequence in which I subjected the Egyptian Pyramids to a barrage of visual puns. The Great Pyramid stands in a vast plain, so precise framing presented no problems.

◄ These pop-art cushions immediately suggested a pose for the model. I could have created a more precise echo, using shoes and stockings, but this one seemed instinctively right, emphasizing the difference between cartoon sex object and flesh-and-blood nude. The photograph and chess table provided a secondary, deliberately more mysterious, juxtaposition.

▲ A writer of prose or poetry might have mentioned haircurlers in a simile or metaphor to describe this sculpted coiffure. Photographers have the power to bring such comparisons vividly to life. This shot took time to set up, but the effort was well worthwhile. The teacup strengthens the impression of humble domesticity, which contrasts with the aristocratic context.

PRACTICALITIES

MODEL HIRE
● **Model agencies** offer a wide selection of experienced professional models. New clients are sometimes asked to show a portfolio. Rates are negotiable, varying according to location, type of modeling required (toplessness and nudity cost much more) and the individual model's skills. After using a model from an agency, it is considered unethical to bypass the agent by coming to a private agreement about any future sessions.

● **Model cards** (or 'composites') available from model agencies include photographs of the model with accompanying information about their attributes. Treat them with some caution: hair style or color may have changed since the card was produced, or skin blemishes may have been retouched on the photographs. When arranging a nude session, ask about sunbathing marks or operation scars.

● **Modeling schools** are a less expensive source of models than the agencies, and sometimes may waive fees in exchange for quality enlargements.

● **A model release form** is necessary if you plan to sell, exhibit or publish any of your pictures. Signed by the model (or by a parent or guardian if she is not of legal age to execute a contract), this document assigns the photographer copyright in specified photographs in which she appears. Sometimes, certain restrictions of use are stipulated. It is usual for the model to sign the form *after* the session. Blank forms are available from professional photographic bodies, or from some photographic stores.

● **A visiting card** with your name, address and the title 'photographer' is a useful credential.

STUDIO HIRE
● **View the studio** before you hire to check facilities. Note the dimensions, which may affect your choice of lenses. Make sure that the windows can be blacked out, and that changing and makeup facilities are adequate.

● **An extra hire charge** for lighting may be payable, and you will usually have to pay the cost of background paper used. You may also have to pay for the attendance of a technician.

● **Camera clubs** or art schools may be willing to hire out studio space at a competitive rate.

● **Obtain insurance cover** for accidental damage to equipment or injuries to personnel.

CAMERA CLUBS
● **Facilities** offered by clubs vary widely. Ideally you should join one that provides exhibition space, a darkroom, a studio equipped with lights, and programs of instruction.

● **Group modeling sessions,** involving one model and half a dozen or more photographers, are a feature of some clubs. Group sessions have disadvantages: you have little control over lighting, no real rapport with the model, and a limited choice of viewpoints. However, this is a good way to encounter models whom you may be able to hire privately. Sometimes, each photographer in the group is individually allowed a short session with the model.

SELLING YOUR PICTURES
● **A well-prepared presentation** of your best work is essential if you plan to approach magazines or other possible clients. This should preferably take the form of a large portfolio case with plastic envelopes for your prints. A loose-leaf arrangement allows you to edit the selection to suit the needs of your potential client.

● **Before you make a sale,** establish exactly what rights are required: exclusive or non-exclusive, world rights or specified territories.

GLOSSARY

Airbrush. Instrument used by photographers for retouching prints. It uses a controlled flow of compressed air to spray paint or dye.

Aperture. Strictly, the opening that limits the amount of light reaching the film and hence the brightness of the image. In some cameras the aperture is of a fixed size; in others it is in the form of an opening in a barrier called the DIAPHRAGM and can be varied in size. (An iris diaphragm forms a continuously variable opening, while a stop plate has a number of holes of varying sizes.) Photographers, however, generally use the term 'aperture' to refer to the diameter of this opening. See also F-NUMBER.

ASA. American Standards Association, which devised one of the two most commonly used systems for rating the speed of an emulsion (i.e., its sensitivity). A film rated at 400 ASA would be twice as fast as one rated at 200 ASA and four times as fast as one rated at 100 ASA. See also DIN, ISO.

Astigmatism. The inability of a lens to focus vertical and horizontal lines in the same focal plane. Corrected lenses are called 'anastigmatic'.

Automatic camera. Camera that automatically sets the correct exposure by a link between the exposure meter and the shutter or aperture diaphragm or both. There are three main types: aperture priority (the most popular), when the photographer sets the aperture and the camera selects the appropriate speed; shutter priority, when the photographer chooses the speed and the camera sets the correct aperture; and programmed, when the camera sets both aperture and shutter speed. Multi-mode cameras can be set to aperture or shutter priority, and, in some models, programmed.

Autowinder. A mechanism that advances film automatically after you have taken a picture.

Available light. Term used to describe existing light, without the introduction of any supplementary light by the photographer. Usually it refers to low illumination levels, for example indoors or at night.

Backlighting. Lighting, natural or artificial, from behind the subject of a photograph. Because contrast tends to be high, judgment of exposure can be difficult in backlit scenes. An average exposure meter reading over the whole scene will often produce under-exposure, so it is advisable to take also a separate reading for the part of the subject for which normal exposure is required. Backlighting can often be used to create a special effect; for example, a pure silhouetted shape, or a halo around a model's head.

Back projection. Projection of transparencies from behind, instead of onto the front of, a reflective screen.

Ball-and-socket head. Type of tripod fitting that allows the camera to be secured at the required angle by fastening a single locking-screw. See also PAN-AND-TILT HEAD.

Barndoors. Hinged flaps mounted on the front of studio lamps to control the direction of light and the width of the beam.

Barrel distortion. Lens defect characterized by the distortion of straight lines at the edges of an image so that they curve inwards at the corners of the frame.

Beaded screen. Type of front-projection screen. The surface of the screen is covered with minute glass beads, giving a brighter picture than a plain white screen.

Bellows. Light-tight folding bag made of pleated cloth used on some cameras to join the lens to the camera body.

Between-the-lens shutter. One of the two main types of shutter. Situated close to the diaphragm, it consists of thin metal blades or leaves which spring open and then close when the camera is fired, exposing the film. See also FOCAL-PLANE SHUTTER.

Bloom. Thin coating of metallic fluoride on the air-glass surface of a lens. It reduces reflections at that surface.

Bounced flash. Soft light achieved by aiming flash at a wall or ceiling to avoid the harsh shadows that result if the light is pointed directly at the subject.

Bracketing. Technique of ensuring optimum exposure by taking several identical pictures of the same subject at slightly different exposure settings. Bracketing is used in tricky, non-average lighting situations (backlit scenes, snowscapes, sunsets), particularly when the EXPOSURE LATITUDE of the film is small.

B setting. Setting of the shutter speed dial of a camera at which the shutter remains open for as long as the release button is held down, allowing longer exposures than the pre-set speeds on the camera. The 'B' stands for 'brief' or 'bulb' (for historical reasons). See also T SETTING.

Burning in. Technique used in printing photographs when a small area of the print requires more exposure than the rest. After normal exposure the main area is shielded with a card or by the hands while the detail (e.g., a highlight which is too dense on the negative) receives further exposure. See also DODGING.

Cable release. Simple camera accessory used to reduce camera vibrations when the shutter is released, particularly when the camera is supported by a tripod and a relatively long exposure is being used. It consists of a short length of thin cable attached at one end to the shutter release of the camera; the cable is encased in a flexible rubber or metal tube and is operated by a plunger.

Camera movements. Adjustments to the relative positions of the lens and the film whereby the geometry of the image can be controlled. A full range of movements is a particular feature of view cameras, though a few smaller cameras allow limited movements, and special lenses are available which do the same for 35mm cameras.

Camera shake. Accidental movement of the camera during exposure, resulting in overall blurring of the photographic image. The main causes are pressing the shutter release too vigorously and hand-holding the camera while shooting at slow shutter speeds.

Cassette. Container for 35mm film. After exposure the film is wound back onto the spool of the cassette before the camera is opened.

Cast. Overall shift towards a particular hue, giving color photographs an unnatural appearance.

CdS cell. Photosensitive cell used in one type of light meter, incorporating a cadmium sulphide resistor, which regulates an electric current. See also SELENIUM CELL.

Center-weighted meter. Type of through-the-lens light meter. The reading is most strongly influenced by the intensity of light at the center of the image.

Chromatic aberration. The inability of a lens to focus different colors on the same focal plane.

Color compensating filters. Filters designated by the letters CC and used to alter the color balance of a slide, particularly to compensate for a color bias in the light source.

Color conversion filters. Filters used to adjust the color balance of a light source when it differs substantially from the color temperature for which a film type is designed. Such filters can convert tungsten slide film into daylight film or vice versa.

Color correction filters (or light balancing filters). Comparatively weak color filters used to correct for small differences between the color temperature of the illumination used for a particular exposure and that for which the film was manufactured. An 85B filter is used with tungsten film in daylight, an 80A filter with daylight film in tungsten light. The name is also sometimes rather loosely employed to describe the cyan, magenta and yellow filters that are used in an enlarger to balance the color of prints made from color negatives or color transparencies.

Color negative film. Film yielding color negatives intended for printing.

Color reversal film. Film yielding color positives (i.e., slides or transparencies) directly. Prints can also be made from the positive transparencies.

Color temperature. Measure of the relative blueness or redness of a light source, expressed in KELVINS. The color temperature is the temperature to which a theoretical 'black body' would have to be heated to give out light of the same color.

Complementary colors. Two contrasting colors that produce an achromatic shade (white, gray or black) when mixed. In color films and color printing processes, the most important pairs are red-cyan, green-magenta and blue-yellow.

Compound lens. Lens consisting of more than one element, designed so that the faults of the various elements largely cancel each other out.

Contact print. Print which is the same size as the negative, made by sandwiching together the negative and the photographic paper when making the print.

Contrast. Degree of difference between the lightest and darkest parts of a subject, negative, print or slide.

Contre jour. Alternative term for BACKLIGHTING. (French for 'against the light'.)

Converging verticals. Distorted appearance of vertical lines in the image, produced when the camera is tilted upward; tall objects such as buildings appear to be leaning backward. Can be partially corrected at the printing stage, or by the use of CAMERA MOVEMENTS.

Converter. See TELECONVERTER.

Covering power. The largest image area of acceptable quality that a given lens produces. The covering power of a lens is normally only slightly greater than the standard negative size for which it is intended, except in the case of a lens designed for use on a camera with movements (see CAMERA MOVEMENTS), when the covering power must be considerably greater.

Cropping. Enlarging only a selected portion of the negative.

Daylight film. Color film balanced to give accurate color rendering in average daylight, that is to say, when the COLOR TEMPERATURE of the light source is around 5,500 kelvins. Also suitable for use with flash.

Dedicated flash. Flash unit made for one specific model or range of cameras to enable light output, aperture and shutter speed to be synchronized perfectly.

Definition. Sharpness of detail and general clarity of a photograph. Definition depends on several factors – accurate focusing, the quality and resolving power of the lens and the speed of the emulsion.

Depth of field. Zone of acceptable sharpness extending in front of and behind the point on the subject which is exactly focused by the lens. Depth of field varies with (1) the distance of the point focused from the lens (the shorter the distance, the more shallow the depth of field); (2) the size of the aperture (the smaller the aperture, the greater the depth of field); (3) the focal length of the lens (the greater the focal length, the shallower the depth of field). The zone of sharpness behind the point focused is greater than that in front of the point. Many modern SLRs using open-aperture exposure metering also have a depth of field preview button that closes the lens diaphragm to the f-number selected and enables the depth of field to be assessed on the viewing screen. The drawback of this method is that the screen darkens progressively as the diaphragm is closed. SLRs using stop-down metering automatically give depth of field preview, as metering can be done only at the selected aperture and not at full aperture.

Depth of focus. Very narrow zone on the image side of the lens within which slight variations in the position of the film will make no appreciable difference to the focusing of the image.

Developer. Chemical agent which converts the LATENT IMAGE into a visible image.

Diaphragm. System of adjustable metal blades forming a roughly circular opening of variable diameter, used to control the APERTURE of a lens.

Diapositive. Alternative name for TRANSPARENCY.

Diffraction. Phenomenon occurring when light passes close to the edge of an opaque body or through a narrow aperture. The light is slightly deflected, setting up interference patterns which may sometimes be seen by the naked eye as fuzziness. The effect is occasionally noticeable in photography, as when, for example, a very small lens aperture is used.

Diffusion. Scattering of light when it is reflected from an uneven surface (diffuse reflection) or when it is transmitted through a translucent but not transparent medium. A reflecting surface does not have to be obviously rough, as even tiny irregularities (as in a layer of seemingly perfectly smooth paint) will scatter the light. The term diffuser, however, usually refers to a medium through which the light is transmitted (tracing paper, for example), rather than to a reflecting surface. Diffusion has the effect of softening light, eliminating glare and harsh shadows. When colored surfaces and media act as diffusers, some of the light is also absorbed.

DIN. Deutsche Industrie Norm, the German standards association, which devised one of the widely used systems for rating the speed of an emulsion (see ASA and ISO). On the DIN scale, every increase of 3 indicates that film sensitivity has doubled. 21 DIN is equivalent to 100 ISO.

Dodging. Technique, also known as shading, used in printing photographs when one area of the print requires less exposure than the rest. A hand or a sheet of card is used to prevent the selected area from receiving the full exposure. See also BURNING IN.

Dolly. Mobile support on wheels, used in the studio with large-format cameras and with lights.

Dry mounting. Method of mounting prints onto card backing, using a special heat-sensitive adhesive tissue that is placed between the print and card and bonds them when they are placed in a hot press.

Effects light. A light introduced into a picture for a specific creative effect, rather than as part of the overall lighting scheme.

Electronic flash. Type of flashgun which uses the flash of light produced by a high-voltage electrical discharge between two electrodes in a gas-filled tube.

Emulsion. In photography, the light-sensitive layer of a photographic material. The emulsion consists essentially of silver halide crystals suspended in a layer of GELATIN.

Enlargement. Photographic print larger than the original image on the film. See also CONTACT PRINT.

Exposure. Total amount of light allowed to reach the light-sensitive material during the formation of the LATENT IMAGE. The exposure is dependent on the brightness of the image, the camera APERTURE and on the length of time for which the photographic material is exposed.

Exposure latitude. Tolerance of photographic material to variations in exposure.

Exposure meter. Instrument for measuring the intensity of light so as to determine the correct SHUTTER and APERTURE settings. The basic principle is that of light energizing a photosensitive cell to produce a current that actuates a pointer or LEDS.

Extension tubes. Accessories used in close-up photography, consisting of metal tubes that can be fitted between the lens and the camera body, thus increasing the lens-to-film distance.

Fast lens. Lens of wide maximum aperture, relative to its focal length. The current state of lens design and manufacture determines the standards by which a lens is judged 'fast' for its focal length.

Fill-in light. Additional lighting used to supplement the principal light source and brighten shadows. Fill-in light can be supplied by redirecting light with a white cardboard or metal foil reflector, as well as by supplementary lamps or flash units.

Film speed. A film's degree of sensitivity to light. Usually expressed as a rating on the ISO, ASA or the DIN scales.

Filter. Transparent sheet, usually of glass or gelatin, used to block a specific part of the light passing through it, or to change or distort the image in some way. See also COLOR CONVERSION FILTERS, COLOR CORRECTION FILTERS, and POLARIZING FILTERS.

Fisheye lens. Extreme wide-angle lens, with an angle of view of about 180°. Since its DEPTH OF FIELD is almost infinite, there is no need for any focusing, but it produces images that are highly distorted.

Flare. Light reflected inside the camera or between the elements of the lens, giving rise to irregular marks on the negative and degrading the quality of the image. It is to some extent overcome by using bloomed lenses (see BLOOM).

Flashbulb. Expendable bulb with a filament of metal foil which is designed to burn up very rapidly giving a brief, intense flare of light, sufficiently bright to allow a photograph to be taken. Most flashbulbs have a light blue plastic coating, which gives the flash a COLOR TEMPERATURE close to that of daylight. Except in simple cameras, flashbulbs are now being superseded by electronic flashguns, some of them automatic.

Flash exposure meter. An exposure meter designed to read only the light from flash sources and ignore all other types of light. The photographer holds the meter close to the subject and points it at the flash, which when fired causes a needle to swing across a scale or one of a series of diodes to light up on the meter.

Floodlight. General term for artificial light source which provides a constant and continuous output of light, suitable for studio photography or similar work. Usually consists of a 125–500W tungsten-filament lamp mounted in a reflector.

F-number. Number resulting when the focal length of a lens is divided by the diameter of the aperture. A sequence of f-numbers, marked on the ring or dial which controls the diaphragm, is used to calibrate the aperture in regular steps (known as STOPS) between its smallest and largest settings. The f-numbers generally follow a standard sequence such that the interval between one stop and the next represents a halving or doubling in the image brightness. As f-numbers represent fractions, the numbers become progressively higher as the aperture is reduced to allow in less light.

Focal length. Distance between the optical center of a lens and the point at which rays of light parallel to the optical axis are brought to a focus. In general, the greater the focal length of a lens, the smaller its angle of view.

Focal plane. Plane on which a given subject is brought to a sharp focus. In practical terms, this means the plane where the film is positioned.

Focal-plane shutter. One of the two main types of shutter, used almost universally in SINGLE-LENS REFLEX CAMERAS. Positioned behind the lens (though in fact slightly in front of the focal plane) the shutter consists of a system of cloth blinds or metal blades; when the camera is fired, a slit travels across the image area either vertically or horizontally. The width and speed of travel of the slit determine the duration of the exposure.

Focusing screen. Screen of glass or plastic mounted in a camera to allow viewing and focusing of the image that the lens forms. Ground glass focusing screens are used principally in large-format cameras. SLR cameras usually have a FRESNEL LENS incorporated in their focusing screens, together with one or more focusing aids, typically in the form of a microprism collar and/or a split-image rangefinder device. Some SLR cameras have interchangeable focusing screens suited to specialist subjects or the photographer's individual preferences.

Format. The size or shape of a negative or print. The term generally refers to a particular film size (e.g., 35mm), but in its more general sense can mean simply whether a picture is upright (vertical) or longitudinal (horizontal).

Fresnel lens. Lens whose surface consists of a series of concentric circular 'steps', each of which is shaped like part of the surface of a convex lens. Fresnel lenses are often used in the viewing screens of single-lens reflex cameras and for spotlights.

Frontlighting. A form of lighting in which the principal light source shines from the direction of the camera toward the subject.

Front projection. A technique of projecting an image onto the front of a screen to provide a suitable background for a subject placed in front of it. This can be done with an ordinary slide projector or, more easily, with a special front projection unit, which eliminates unwanted shadows.

Gelatin. Colloid material used as binding medium for the emulsion of photographic paper and film; also used in some types of filter.

Grain. Granular texture appearing to some degree in all processed photographic materials. In black-and-white photographs the grains are minute particles of black metallic silver which constitute the dark areas of a photograph. In color photographs the silver has been removed chemically, but tiny blotches of dye retain the appearance of graininess. Grain usually increases with film speed. It can be used for arresting pictorial effects.

Gray card. Card of a standard reflectance, used to obtain average reflected-light exposure readings.

Guide number. Number indicating the effective power of a flash unit. For a given film speed, the guide number divided by the distance between the flash and the subject gives the appropriate F-NUMBER to use.

Hard light. Strong, direct light that has not been diffused in any way. Hard light produces sharp, dense shadows and models forms clearly. It makes strong colors appear more brilliant and weakens pale colors.

High-key. Containing predominantly light tones. See also LOW-KEY.

Highlights. Brightest areas of the subject, or corresponding areas of an image; in a negative these are areas of greatest density.

Honeycomb. Mesh-like studio lighting attachment designed to create a sharp, narrow beam, without light spillage.

Hotshoe. Accessory shoe on a camera which incorporates a live contact for firing a flashgun, thus eliminating the need for a separate socket.

Hue. The quality that distinguishes between colors of the same saturation and brightness; the quality, for example, of redness or greenness.

Hyperfocal distance. Shortest distance at which a lens can be focused to give a depth of field extending to infinity.

Incident light. Light falling on the subject. When a subject is being photographed, readings may be taken of the incident light instead of the reflected light.

Instant camera. Camera that produces more-or-less instantaneous pictures by using a 'sandwich' of film, processing chemicals and printing paper.

IR (infrared) setting. A mark sometimes found on the focusing ring of a camera, indicating a shift in focus needed for infrared photography.

ISO (International Standards Organization). System of rating emulsion speeds which is replacing ASA and DIN. ISO 100 corresponds to 100 ASA.

Joule. Unit of energy in the SI (Système International) system of units. The joule is used in photography to indicate the output of an electronic flash.

Kelvin (K). Unit of temperature in the SI system of units. The kelvin scale begins at absolute zero ($-273°C$) and uses degrees equal in magnitude to $1°C$. Kelvins are used in photography to express COLOR TEMPERATURE.

Key light. The main source of light in any lighting setup, determining the overall character of the illumination.

Latent image. Invisible image recorded on photographic emulsion as a result of exposure to light. The latent image is converted into a visible image by the action of a DEVELOPER.

LCD (Liquid crystal display). Electronic numerical indicator that displays shutter speeds and apertures in the viewfinder of certain SLR cameras, relating directly to the camera's exposure control. LCD systems, which are also used in other photographic apparatus such as handheld exposure meters, have the advantage over LEDs of using less battery power but the disadvantages of being less easily visible in dim lighting conditions and suffering in temperature extremes.

LED (Light emitting diode). Solid state electrical component used as a glowing colored indicator inside a camera viewfinder or other photographic apparatus to provide a visual signal or warning indicator for various controls. The most common use of LEDs is to provide exposure information in viewfinders. This is done most simply by a light glowing when exposure is correct, and in its most sophisticated form by a display of digital figures indicating aperture, shutter speed and other factors such as whether flash is being used.

Lens hood. Simple lens accessory, usually made of rubber or light metal, used to shield the lens from light coming from areas outside the field of view. Such light is the source of FLARE.

Light balancing filters. See COLOR CORRECTION FILTERS.

Long-focus lens. Lens of focal length greater than that of the STANDARD LENS for a given format. Long-focus lenses have a narrow field of view, and consequently make distant objects appear closer. See also TELEPHOTO LENS.

Low-key. Containing predominantly dark tones. See also HIGH-KEY.

Macro lens. Strictly, a lens capable of giving a 1:1 magnification ratio (a lifesize image); the term is generally used to describe any close-focusing lens. Macro lenses can also be used at ordinary subject distances.

Medium-format camera. Term applied to cameras taking rollfilm and producing a negative or

transparency between approximately 6 × 4.5cm and 6 × 9cm. There are three main kinds: (1) the single-lens reflex, of which there are types used at both waist and eye level; (2) the twin-lens reflex; (3) non-reflex models, the most popular type of which is rather like an enlarged 35mm rangefinder camera except that its lens panel is fitted to extensible bellows.

Mercury vapor lamp. Type of light source sometimes used in studio photography, giving a bluish light. The light is produced by passing an electric current through a tube filled with mercury vapour.

Microprism. Special type of focusing screen composed of a grid of tiny prisms, often incorporated into the viewing screens of SLR cameras. The microprism gives a fragmented appearance when the image is out of focus.

Mired. Acronym for Micro-Reciprocal Degree. Unit on a scale of COLOR TEMPERATURE used to calibrate COLOR CORRECTION FILTERS. The mired value of a light source is equivalent to one million ÷ color temperature in Kelvins.

Mirror lens. Long-focus lens of extremely compact design whose construction is based on a combination of lenses and curved mirrors. Light rays from the subject are reflected backward and forward inside the barrel of the lens before reaching the film plane. Mirror lenses have a fixed aperture, typically f/8 for a 500mm lens. Also known as a catadioptric lens. See also NEUTRAL DENSITY (ND) FILTERS.

Modeling light. A tungsten lamp mounted close to the flash tube of a studio flash unit. The continuous illumination of the modelling light simulates the effect that will be produced by the instantaneous burst of the flash, and is thus useful for previewing the lighting of a picture.

Montage. Composite photographic image made from several different pictures by physically assembling them or printing them successively onto a single piece of paper.

Motordrive. Battery-operated device that attaches to a camera and automatically advances the film and re-tensions the shutter after an exposure has been made. Some motordrives can advance the film at speeds of up to five frames per second.

Negative. Image in which light tones are recorded as dark, and vice versa; in color negatives every color in the original subject is represented by its COMPLEMENTARY COLOR.

Neutral density (ND) filter. Uniformly gray filter which reduces the brightness of an image without altering its color content. Used in conjunction with lenses that have no diaphragm to control the aperture (such as MIRROR LENSES), or when the light is too bright for the speed of film used.

Normal lens. See STANDARD LENS.

Off-camera flash. Small flash unit linked to the camera with an electrical lead. Off-camera flash enables you to create more varied lighting effects than does a flashgun fitted to the hotshoe of the camera.

Open flash. Technique of firing flash manually after the camera shutter has been opened instead of synchronizing the two.

Orthochromatic. Term used to describe the black-and-white emulsions that are insensitive to red light. See also PANCHROMATIC.

Pan-and-tilt head. Type of tripod head employing independent locking mechanisms for movement in two planes at right angles to

each other. Thus the camera can be locked in one plane while remaining free to move in the other.

Panchromatic. Term used to describe black-and-white photographic emulsions that are sensitive to all the visible colors (although not uniformly so). Most modern films are panchromatic. See also ORTHOCHROMATIC.

Panning. Technique of swinging the camera to follow a moving subject, used to convey the impression of speed. A relatively slow shutter speed is used, so that a sharp image of the moving object is recorded against a blurred background.

Parallax. Apparent displacement of an object brought about by a change of viewpoint. Parallax error, apparent in close-ups only, is the discrepancy between the image produced by the lens and the view seen through the viewfinder in cameras where the viewfinder and taking lens are separate.

Pentaprism. Five-sided prism used in the construction of eye-level viewfinders for SLR cameras, providing a laterally correct, upright image. (In practice many pentaprisms have more than five sides, since unnecessary parts of the prism are cut off to reduce its bulk.)

Photo-electric cell. Light-sensitive cell used in the circuit of a light meter. Some types of photo-electric cell generate an electric current when stimulated by light; others react by a change in their electrical resistance.

Photoflood (photolamp). Bright tungsten filament bulb used as an artificial light source in photography. The bulb is over-run and so has a short life.

Polarized light. Light whose electrical vibrations are confined to a single plane. In everyday conditions, light is usually unpolarized, having electrical (and magnetic) vibrations in every plane. However, light reflected from shiny non-metallic surfaces is frequently polarized, making it difficult for us to distinguish color and detail. This effect can be controlled with a POLARIZING FILTER.

Polarizing filter. Thin transparent filter used as a lens accessory to cut down reflections from certain shiny surfaces (notably glass and water) or to intensify the color of a blue sky. Polarizing filters are made of a material that will polarize light passing through it and which will also block a proportion of light that has already been polarized; rotating the filter will vary the proportion that is blocked.

Positive. Image in which the light tones correspond to the light areas of the subject, and the dark tones correspond to the dark areas; in a positive color image, the colors of the subject are also represented by the same colors in the image. See also NEGATIVE.

Primary colors. Blue, green and red – the colors of light that when mixed together equally make white light and that when mixed in various combinations can make any other color. Saturated colors are 'pure' colors that reflect only one or two primaries; when a third primary is introduced, the color is 'desaturated' toward white, gray or black.

Pushing. Technique of extending the development of a film so as to increase its effective speed or to improve contrast. Usually used after rating a film at a higher than normal speed.

Rangefinder. Optical device for measuring distance, often coupled to the focusing mechanism of a camera lens. A rangefinder displays two images, showing the scene from slightly different viewpoints, which must be superimposed to establish the measurement of distance.

Reciprocity failure. The occurrence of an unwanted color cast in an image due to an extremely long, or (less often) extremely short, exposure.

Red eye. The bright red color of the pupil of the eye that sometimes disfigures pictures taken by flash. It is caused by reflection of the flash unit's light from layers of the retina rich in blood vessels. Red eye can be avoided by making sure the subject is not looking directly at the camera or by using OFF-CAMERA FLASH or BOUNCED FLASH.

Reflector. Any surface capable of reflecting light; in photography, generally understood to mean sheets of white, gray or silvered material used to reflect light into shadow areas. Lamp reflectors are generally dish-shaped mirrors, with the lamp recessed into the concave interior, which points toward the subject. Studio electronic flash equipment is often combined with an umbrella reflector, usually silvered, mounted on a stand.

Reflex camera. Generic name for types of camera whose viewing systems employ a mirror to reflect an image onto a screen. See TWIN-LENS REFLEX CAMERA and SINGLE-LENS REFLEX CAMERA.

Refraction. Bending of a ray of light traveling obliquely from one medium to another; the ray is refracted at the surface of the two media. The angle through which a ray will be bent can be calculated from the refractive indices of the media.

Resolving power. Ability of an optical system to distinguish between objects that are very close together; also used in photography to describe this ability in a film or paper emulsion.

Rimlighting. Lighting arrangement, principally used in portraiture, in which the light comes from behind or above the subject, creating a bright rim of light around the outline.

Ring flash. A circular flash unit fitted around the lens, used for even, shadowless lighting in close-up photography and sometimes in portraiture.

Sandwiching. The projection or printing of two or more slides together to produce a composite image.

Saturated color. Pure color, free from any admixture of gray.

Selective focusing. Technique of using shallow DEPTH OF FIELD at a wide aperture setting to show parts of a scene in sharp focus while other parts are deliberately blurred.

Selenium cell. One of the principal types of photo-electric cell used in light meters. A selenium cell produces a current when stimulated by light, proportional to the intensity of the light. Selenium-cell meters do not require batteries.

Shading. Alternative term for DODGING.

Shutter. Camera mechanism which controls the duration of the exposure. The two principal types of shutter are BETWEEN-THE-LENS SHUTTERS and FOCAL-PLANE SHUTTERS.

Sidelighting. A form of lighting in which light falls on the subject from one side. Sidelighting produces dramatic effects, casting long shadows and emphasizing texture and form.

Single-lens reflex (SLR) camera. One of the most popular types of camera design. Its name derives from its viewfinder system, which enables the user to see the image produced by the same lens that is used for taking the photograph. A hinged mirror reflects this image onto a viewing screen, where the picture may be composed and focused; when the shutter is released, the mirror flips out of the light path while the film is being exposed.

Skylight filter. A pale filter that helps to cut down the amount of blue light entering the camera. This attachment, which is similar to a UV filter, is useful when photographing scenes containing a lot of sky.

Slave unit. Photo-electric device used to trigger electronic flash units in studio work. The slave unit detects light from a primary flashgun linked directly to the camera, and instantaneously fires the secondary flash unit to which it is connected.

Slide copier (duplicator). A device used to make duplicates of transparencies. Bench-top copiers incorporate a lens, a built-in light source, a camera mount and a slide holder. A simpler copy tube allows you to use the camera lens and a portable flash unit.

SLR. Abbreviation of SINGLE-LENS REFLEX CAMERA.

Snoot. A conical attachment fitted to a studio light to concentrate the beam.

Soft focus. Deliberately diffused or blurred definition of an image, often used to create a dreamy, romantic look in portraiture. Soft-focus effects are often achieved with special filters, engraved so that the glass surface breaks up the light by means of refraction.

Soft light. Light that has lost its intensity by being diffused or reflected. Soft light produces weak shadows and reveals fine detail and textures.

Speed. The sensitivity of an emulsion as measured on one of the various scales (see ASA, ISO and DIN); or the maximum aperture of which a given lens is capable.

Spherical aberration. Lens defect resulting in an unsharp image, caused by light rays passing through the outer edges of a lens being more strongly refracted than those passing through the central parts; not all rays, therefore, are brought to exactly the same focus.

Spotlight. Lamp unit designed to emit a concentrated beam of light. Spotlights have clear lamps and polished reflectors (usually a hemispherical concave mirror), and are often fitted with a FRESNEL LENS, which is lightweight and heat resistant, and throws a beam of evenly directed light.

Spot meter. Special type of light meter which takes a reading from a very narrow angle of view; in some TTL METERS the reading may be taken from only a small central position of the image in the viewfinder.

Spotting. Retouching a print or negative to remove spots and blemishes.

Standard lens. Lens of focal length approximately equal to the diagonal of the negative format for which it is intended. In the case of 35mm cameras the standard lens usually has a focal length in the range of 50–55mm, slightly greater than the actual diagonal of a full-frame negative (about 43mm).

Stop. Alternative name for aperture setting or F-NUMBER.

Stopping down. Colloquial term for reducing the aperture of the lens. See also STOP.

Sync lead. Electrical lead used to link the camera to a flashgun for OFF-CAMERA FLASH.

Teleconverter. Device that fits between a lens and camera body to increase the effective focal length of the lens and produce a magnified image. Teleconverters come in various 'strengths', typically × 2 or × 3, and reduce the effective F-NUMBER of the lens proportionally.

Telephoto lens. Strictly, a special type of LONG-FOCUS LENS, having an optical construction which consists of two lens groups. The front

group acts as a converging system, while the rear group diverges the light rays. This construction results in the lens being physically shorter than its effective focal length. Most long-focus lenses are now of telephoto construction.

Test strip. Print showing the effects of several trial exposure times, made in order to establish the correct exposure for the final print.

Thyristor control. Computer flash device used to conserve unspent energy and enable faster and more economical recycling of a flash unit.

TLR. Abbreviation of TWIN-LENS REFLEX CAMERA.

Toner. Chemical used to alter the color of a black-and-white print. There are four principal types of toner, each requiring a different process for treating the print. Almost any color can be achieved.

Transparency. A photograph viewed by transmitted, rather than reflected, light. When mounted in a rigid frame, the transparency is called a slide.

T setting. Abbreviation of 'time' setting – a mark on some shutter controls. The T setting is used for long exposures when the photographer wishes to leave the camera with its shutter open. The first time the shutter release is pressed, the shutter opens; it remains open until the release is pressed a second time. See also B SETTING.

TTL (through-the-lens) meter. Built-in exposure meter which measures the intensity of light in the image produced by the main camera lens. Principally found in the more sophisticated designs of SINGLE-LENS REFLEX CAMERAS.

Tungsten halogen lamp. Type of tungsten lamp in which the glass envelope through which the filament runs contains a halogen gas (usually iodine and/or bromine). The halogen enables the lamp to maintain its color quality throughout its life by preventing vaporized tungsten from migrating to the envelope and thereby causing blackening.

Tungsten light. A common type of electric light for both household and photographic purposes, named after the filament of the metal tungsten through which the current passes. Tungsten light is much warmer in color (more orange) than daylight or electronic flash, and with daylight-balanced slide film you must use a blue filter to reproduce colors accurately. Alternatively, you can use special tungsten-balanced slide film.

Twin-lens reflex (TLR) camera. Type of camera whose viewing system employs a secondary lens of focal length equal to that of the main 'taking' lens: a fixed mirror reflects the image from the viewing lens up onto a ground-glass screen. Twin-lens reflex cameras suffer from PARALLAX error, particularly when focused at close distances, owing to the difference in position between the viewing lens and the taking lens. See also SINGLE-LENS REFLEX CAMERA.

UV filter. Filter used over the camera lens to absorb ultraviolet radiation, which is particularly prevalent on hazy days. A UV filter enables the photographer to penetrate the haze to some extent. UV filters, having no effect on the exposure, are sometimes kept permanently in position over the lens to protect it from damage.

View camera. Large-format studio camera whose viewing system consists of a ground-glass screen at the back of the camera on which the picture is composed and focused before the film is inserted. The front and back of the camera are attached by a flexible bellows unit, which allows a full range of CAMERA MOVEMENTS.

Viewfinder. Window or frame on a camera, showing the scene that will appear in the picture, and often incorporating a RANGEFINDER mechanism.

Vignette. Picture printed in such a way that the image fades gradually into the border area.

Virtual image. In optics, an image that cannot be obtained on a screen; a virtual image is seen in a position through which rays of light appear to have passed but in fact have not.

Wide-angle lens. Lens of focal length shorter than that of a STANDARD LENS, and consequently having a wider angle of view.

Window light. A studio flash unit with a built-in diffuser in the form of a rectangular acrylic sheet.

Zone focusing. Technique of presetting the aperture and focusing of the camera so that the entire zone in which the subject is likely to appear is covered by the DEPTH OF FIELD.

Zoom lens. Lens of variable FOCAL LENGTH whose focusing remains unchanged while its focal length is being altered. Zooming is accomplished by changing the relative positions of some of the elements within the lens. Some zoom lenses have separate control rings for focusing and zooming, while on other designs a single ring serves for both purposes (twisting the ring focuses the lens, pushing or pulling it changes the focal length). The latter type is generally known as 'one-touch'. Various ranges of focal lengths are available in zoom lenses. Most typically, they extend from wide-angle/standard (say, 28–50mm); moderate wide-angle or standard/moderate telephoto (35–70mm or 50–135mm); or moderate/long telephoto (80–200mm). Zooms are heavier and have smaller maximum apertures than ordinary lenses.

SESSION NOTES

A successful day's shooting depends partly upon advance planning. Use the note pages that follow as a combined photo diary and checklist. For each session, itemize the timing and travel arrangements, the equipment, props and other items that need to be assembled beforehand, and the picture ideas you want to try. Although some photographers record every detail of exposure, filtration and processing for each picture they take, I personally find this too time-consuming. However, it is certainly worth making detailed notes if you are trying out special effects or new techniques. When the note pages are full, start a new photo notebook, adapting the format if necessary to suit your specific needs.

Job number *120*   Date *Tues. June 5*   Time *All day. pick up J. 9am 23 Rose Lane*

Model *Janice Creeley*

Agent —

Location *Pagoda, Lee Park*

Meal arrangements *Lunch, Flying Duck Rest., 1.30 643 87290*

Equipment *Nikon kit, soft-focus and pol. filters, tripod, 28mm, 50mm, 100mm lenses, 2× conv.*

Lighting *2 portable flash, slave unit, Lastolite reflectors*

Film *Kodachrome 64 (6×36), Ekt. 200 (4×36)*

Clothes *Kimono, Japanese comb, wooden sandals*

Makeup *Pale, oriental*

Props *Parasol, hand mirror, shrimping net, tea set, jewelry*

Picture plans *Door of pagoda, edge of pond, tea ceremony*

Notes *Pushed Ekt. rolls 3 and 4, 2 stops. Prints promised to J — esp. paddling pix. Very spontaneous. Graceful movements, good posture. Legs a little dumpy.*

Job number   Date   Time

Model

Agent

Location

Meal arrangements

Equipment

Lighting

Film

Clothes

Makeup

Props

Picture plans

Notes

Job number   Date   Time

Model

Agent

Location

Meal arrangements

Equipment

Lighting

Film

Clothes

Makeup

Props

Picture plans

Notes

Job number   Date   Time

Model

Agent

Location

Meal arrangements

Equipment

Lighting

Film

Clothes

Makeup

Props

Picture plans

Notes

Job number   Date   Time

Model

Agent

Location

Meal arrangements

Equipment

Lighting

Film

Clothes

Makeup

Props

Picture plans

Notes

Job number   Date   Time

Model

Agent

Location

Meal arrangements

Equipment

Lighting

Film

Clothes

Makeup

Props

Picture plans

Notes

Job number   Date   Time

Model

Agent

Location

Meal arrangements

Equipment

Lighting

Film

Clothes

Makeup

Props

Picture plans

Notes

Job number   Date   Time

Model

Agent

Location

Meal arrangements

Equipment

Lighting

Film

Clothes

Makeup

Props

Picture plans

Notes

Job number   Date   Time

Model

Agent

Location

Meal arrangements

Equipment

Lighting

Film

Clothes

Makeup

Props

Picture plans

Notes

Job number   Date   Time

Model

Agent

Location

Meal arrangements

Equipment

Lighting

Film

Clothes

Makeup

Props

Picture plans

Notes

Job number   Date   Time

Model

Agent

Location

Meal arrangements

Equipment

Lighting

Film

Clothes

Makeup

Props

Picture plans

Notes

Job number   Date   Time

Model

Agent

Location

Meal arrangements

Equipment

Lighting

Film

Clothes

Makeup

Props

Picture plans

Notes

MODEL PROFILES

Model

Address

Telephone
Agent

Physical attributes

Notes

Model

Address

Telephone
Agent

Physical attributes

Notes

Model

Address

Telephone
Agent

Physical attributes

Notes

Model

Address

Telephone
Agent

Physical attributes

Notes

Model

Address

Telephone
Agent

Physical attributes

Notes

Model

Address

Telephone
Agent

Physical attributes

Notes

Model

Address

Telephone
Agent

Physical attributes

Notes

Model

Address

Telephone
Agent

Physical attributes

Notes

Model

Address

Telephone
Agent

Physical attributes

Notes

Model

Address

Telephone
Agent

Physical attributes

Notes

Model

Address

Telephone
Agent

Physical attributes

Notes

Model

Address

Telephone
Agent

Physical attributes

Notes

Index

Page numbers in **bold** type refer to main entries